On Borrowed Time

On Borrowed Time

How I Built a Life While Beating Death

BRYAN R. DONAHUE
WITH M. RUTLEDGE McCALL

2POINT2 LLC
North Haven, CT

Published by
2point2 LLC
North Haven, CT

Publisher's Cataloging-in-Publication Data
Donahue, Bryan R.

    On borrowed time : how I built a life while beating death / Bryan R. Donahue with M. Rutledge McCall. – North Haven, CT : 2point2, 2012.

    p. ; cm.

    ISBN13: 978-0-9860002-0-1

    1. Donahue, Bryan R. 2. Near-death experiences. 3. Life change events. 4. Loan officers—United States—Biography. I. Title. II. McCall, M. Rutledge.

    CT275.A3 D66 2012
    920.00905—dc23   2012937446

FIRST EDITION

Project coordination by Jenkins Group, Inc.
www.BookPublishing.com

Front cover design by Daniel French

Printed in the United States of America
16 15 14 13 12 • 5 4 3 2 1

Dedication

This book is dedicated to Jeff Agli. My world exists because of you. Your gift made it possible for Lily and me to be on this Earth. Lia, Lily J. and I are forever grateful. Your liver saved me, but the depth of your heart astounds me.

Contents

Foreword

Over the years, I have consulted with dozens of gifted clients around the world on scores of books in many different genres. I thoroughly enjoy what I do for the published authors with whom I am privileged to work. But rarely do I come across a person with the heart, the drive, and the desire to lift up his fellow man like Bryan Donahue. His triumph over a harrowing, near-death experience highlights not just his determination to overcome hardship, but his focus on being a positive example to everyone he encounters.

Bryan's story reveals that by making positive decisions about the way we view and deal with each obstacle we encounter in life, and then standing firmly and consistently by those choices, we can gain victory over every challenge and build a great life. Bryan's experience proves that we do have a say in how our life will play out: It starts in the mind, with the simple, yet profound, power of thought.

If you sense that you aren't truly living a productive and fulfilling life, if you feel overburdened with daily pressures, then that's where Bryan's story comes in. I believe he beat death for one reason: so that you might be encouraged by how he survived . . . and how his life continues to *thrive* well beyond his victory.

—M. Rutledge McCall

Acknowledgments

Lia and Lily J, you give me purpose and meaning, you are my world. I love you!

My parents, Bob and Milly, I owe you everything from my foundation to my future. I could not imagine more loving and supportive people. You set the ultimate example.

The Aglis: Jeff, Kristy, Alivia (Lala), Sonia (Nunya Business) and Judy you are Irreplaceable!!!

The Martins: Adam, Amy, Grace (CC), Molly (Hot Tamale) and Emma (M&M) your hearts bring love and your personalities bring pure joy to my life.

Joanne Pacelli, you are a second mother to me. Thank you for everything.

The Dickersons: George, Fran, Brian, Lisa and Audrey (Audie) I could not ask for better in-laws. Your support and love are unbelievable.

The Halls: Todd, Melissa, Eva and Luca your support, love and friendship were key ingredients to winning my life.

Jay and Kelly McGuinness your generosity, love, support and loyalty are amazing.

My Doctors: Marshall Kaplan, MD, Richards Rohrer, MD, Jeffrey Cooper, MD, Richard Freeman, MD, Ann Dempsey, P.A. and Karen Curreri, RN, BSN, CCTC, Your talent, courage, compassion and knowledge blow me away. I'm alive because of the care you, your staff and all the hard working people at Tufts Medical Center gave me.

McCall you are simply brilliant. Thanks!

Pop I wish you could have read this.

PROLOGUE:
Ticking Bomb

If you ever want to get fast, first-class service at a hospital, forget the emergency room—walk in the front door and collapse. I hit the floor in a dead faint and was instantly swarmed by orderlies and nurses. They instructed us to go to the ER, but I couldn't move. When I came to, Lia was in tears, crying out for a wheelchair. For the second time in two months, her husband was dying.

They rushed me to a room on 4 North and began running a battery of tests on me. I vomited and passed out on the CAT-scan table. The scan indicated that there was nothing wrong with me.

Even professionals make mistakes.

When I came to, I was in such unbearable pain that I asked the charge nurse not to keep me alive.

"Forty-eight over twenty-six," another nurse called out my blood pressure.

"*What?* The scan says he's okay!"

When your blood pressure is forty-eight over twenty-six, you are below comatose and barely above dead. They gave me a sedative. I passed out. That night, my wife dozed fitfully on a cot next to me. She awoke abruptly every so often and checked to see if my chest was rising and falling. When I awoke early the next morning, the charge nurse was reviewing my charts and lab reports. She became increasingly agitated as she read through the file. She hurried out and returned moments later with a doctor.

The doctor's demeanor was somber as he analyzed the CAT scan and checked my vitals. Suddenly, he dropped everything and told the nurses, "We're taking him in—*now*," and began yanking cords and calling out orders.

He wheeled my bed out of the room and into the elevator, where another doctor jumped on the bed and sliced into me with a scalpel. "Sorry about this," he apologized tersely and ran a line into me. There was no time for anesthetic.

Less than a decade earlier, when I was in the Marine Corps, my closest friend in boot camp had given me some advice that would echo into my future. One day at the end of a particularly grueling week of training, when I was feeling I couldn't take much more, he said to me, "It's all a game, Bryan. Don't let them break you—if you break, *you lose*." On the operating table that day many years later, I fought to recall his words as the anesthetic dragged me under and the world sank away from me.

It's true what they say: When you're at death's door, your whole life flashes before you like a movie. It was a nice picture.

I didn't want it to end.

CHAPTER 1

The Stuff of Heroes

My dad grew up in an era not that long ago where you took off on your bicycle in the morning and you slid back into the front yard around dusk, grimy, worn out and hungry, just in time for dinner. As long as you were home before supper was served, no one questioned you.

But my father's upbringing in Hamden, Connecticut, wasn't as idyllic as it sounds. His dad drank a lot, so he didn't get much direction or guidance and had to fend for himself. There were no positive role models around. It was a pretty rough and tumble existence—the kind of childhood you wouldn't want a kid to have. But that didn't stop my dad from wanting something better out of life. Five days out of high-school in 1966, he became a U.S. Marine. He was eighteen. Army Staff Sergeant Barry Sadler's song, "The Ballad of the Green Berets," a tale of the exploits of America's military, was a huge radio hit that year, along with the hard-charging "96 Tears" by Question Mark and the Mysterians. Two other songs were also playing in heavy rotation that summer, as counterpoints to the looming battle lines being drawn between peace and war: "California Dreamin'" (by the Mamas and the Papas) and The Association's "Cherish" (the number two song that year behind Sadler's monster hit). Just three years earlier, America had violently lost her beloved young president, John F. Kennedy. Now, revolution was in the air, with the country lurching on the precipice between dark forces clamoring for war and a young generation craving peace. The draft was in full swing, providing soldiers for the escalating conflict in Vietnam. The John Wayne movie *The Green Berets* was being filmed, and would become a massive box office success in 1968, just two summers away.

One year before flower power hit its stride, my dad heeded his country's call. By February of 1967, just nine months after he'd joined the Marines, he was in the sweltering middle of nowhere in a jungle in Vietnam, in a ten-man Combined Action Group located outside of Hue City and Phu Bai. The Marines lived with the locals, taking them out on patrols and teaching them how to defend themselves and their villages from the Viet Cong and the North Vietnamese Army. Forget running water, those people had nothing. No radios, no telephones, not even shoes for their feet. And there was my dad, a teenager, barely out of high-school, given a gun and thrust into combat. Then, in February of '68, one fast year after he landed in-country, he was one short village away when one of the bloodiest battles of the Tet Offensive broke out—the infamous Battle of Hue.

From bicycles to bullets in twenty months. He grew up fast. Living in a poverty-stricken, war-torn country, where the people live on the fringe of existence and so close to death you could smell it coming, sets a kid forever. It either gives him the drive to be better, to take advantage of the blessings and opportunities we have in America; or it can do just the opposite.

In March of 1968, my dad came home—physically intact, thank God. He shook off a lot of demons in 'Nam. He went in as a teenage kid, came back changed—and very appreciative of how good we have it here in America.

When he had left the States to go to war, the hippie movement hadn't yet caught on. He was twenty when he landed back in California. The Woodstock generation was in full swing by then, and anti war sentiment was clashing hard against the powers that be. Long hair, beads, paisley, peace, love, psychedelics, pot. It was culture shock all over again. In little more than one fast year it had all bypassed him. He didn't know what to think. All he did know was that he and his Marine Corps uniform and combat medals and battle flags were not welcome. And when America finally bailed out and abandoned Vietnam, he would always wonder, *They sacrificed my life . . . for what?* Things like that can mess with a young man's mind. But my dad was tough going in. And he was tougher coming out. An American hero had been born.

I was cut from that cloth. I would need it.

Thank God for my upbringing.

CHAPTER 2

American Foundation

A farmer who had a quarrelsome family called his sons and told them to lay a bunch of sticks before him. Then, after laying the sticks parallel to one another and binding them, he challenged his sons, one after one, to pick up the bundle and break it. They all tried, but in vain. Then, untying the bundle, he gave them the sticks to break one by one. This they did with the greatest ease. Then said the father, "Thus, my sons, as long as you remain united, you are a match for anything, but differ and separate, and you are undone."

—Aesop (620–560 B.C.), Greek fabulist

I was born in a tight-knit family, the middle child with two sisters in a family-first atmosphere that instilled loyalty, love and honor.

Both of my grandfathers served in the military in World War II. My dad's father was in the Marine Corps. My mother's dad was in the Italian army, fighting under Mussolini against the Allies in World War II. In fact, he was taken prisoner by the British, who taught him how to speak English. Hanging on the walls in my parents' basement was an interesting visual to the possibilities of the impossible: family photos depicting my relatives in Naples, Italy, supporting Italian soldiers on their way to fight against the United States.

In 1945, after my grandfather was released from the British POW camp, he immigrated to America. My mom was born a few years later in Torrington, Connecticut. My grandfather was proud to become an American—a man who, less than a decade earlier, had fought against the very country he now called home. Anything was possible in America.

My grandmother and grandfather were hardworking, no non-sense, industrious people who lived a very quiet life. Their family was small; it was just them and my mom and her two sisters. They didn't have other family or relatives here in America, so they set about creating family and roots and legacy like so many other immigrant families before them who had contributed to building this great nation.

My grandmother possessed a steely determination and quiet grit. When she got a goal in her head, she went for it. She came to America without any language skills whatsoever, yet she learned.

She and my grandfather didn't have much money, yet when they decided they wanted a house, my grandmother went out and got a job at a factory to help my grandfather save up extra money. And they bought a house. They impressed that "can do" attitude upon my mom.

Years later, when my parents purchased their home, it needed tons of work, but they didn't have enough money. My mom lamented to my grandmother, "I wish I could buy new carpeting, but we can't afford it."

"Sure you can afford it," my grandmother insisted in her singsong Italian accent.

"No, I can't," my mom responded.

"Yes you can," my grandmother replied sternly. *"Go get a job."*

That was my grandmother. You went out and you got a job and that was all there was to it. No nonsense. No whining. My grandparents never had a *Poor me, I can't do it* mindset. There was always a way around any challenge. That's what my mom was raised with. There was no time to sit around dwelling on negatives, you just did it. "We can get there" was their credo.

That was their attitude. That became my mother's attitude. That became my attitude.

* * *

My mom and dad met at a church carnival in Hamden, Connecticut, three years after he returned home from Vietnam. They got married in 1973. Amazing how a pretty, Italian girl can inspire a young Marine to settle down.

My parents made a good team. But there was no "luck" involved in how well grounded my sisters and I turned out. My mom's dad had been in a war, my dad's dad had been in a war, and my dad had been in a war. My father knew what a battle life could be for a kid without parental love and guidance, and my mother knew that only a child raised with both parental love and guidance could handle what life throws at us. So they made my sisters and me their top priority, raising us on the core basics: unconditional love, proper discipline and a solid work ethic.

After his service in the Marines, my dad got a job as a letter carrier with the United States Postal Service. Whenever the post office would offer training, he would take advantage of it, eventually gaining certification in several different disciplines, with an emphasis on security positions.

We were a normal, middle-class American family. My father worked nights at the post office, arriving home around six in the morning. An hour later, my mom would leave for her job in the underwriting department of a health insurance company. Dad would take us to school in the morning and would sleep during the day. At three in the afternoon, he'd pick us up after school. Mom would arrive home at four and begin preparing dinner.

My parents worked hard for what they had and didn't live beyond their means. They provided what we needed, and encouraged us to work to earn money for what we wanted. They gave us an option: "If you really want that, fine. But if you spend your money on that, you're not going to have any money for something else later." As kids do, we often spent our money on what we wanted, but in making it our decision, we were learning all about financial responsibility and decision-making.

The way my parents lived their lives demonstrated the importance they placed on individual involvement in each of our lives. My father often took me to sporting events, dinner, movies, etc. When the movie *Rambo* came out, for example, his buddies said,

"Hey Bob, you wanna go see that movie with us?" "Sure," my dad said, "but my son's gotta come with us." He always included me.

One day, I asked him, "Hey, Dad, why don't you ever go out just with your friends?"

"I do," he grinned and tousled my hair.

It took me awhile to get that I was his friend. He wanted to be involved in my life to make sure that I knew I was loved and so I would walk the straight and narrow, because he never had any of that from his dad when he was a boy.

My parents navigated the trials and joys of parenthood as a team, always managing to keep things on track and moving forward. Mom was the glue that held everything in central orbit so nothing went flying off. Dad was the disciplinarian. He never allowed us to get away with anything. He made sure there were rules to follow and consequences for breaking those rules. Dad would tell us what we *had to* do; whereas, Mom would tell us what we *should* do—and then give us a look that was far more effective than Dad's *had to*. Mom rarely got angry or flustered, but her full-blown Italian occasionally would come roaring out and—*WHAP!* She'd slap that wooden spoon down on the countertop and we'd straighten right up and do whatever it was she was suggesting we should do.

Whenever we would mess up when Dad wasn't home, Mom would slowly shake her head in a way that made us realize we were in big trouble when Dad got home. "Your father is going to be *sooo* disappointed with you," she would say in that powerfully soft voice of hers. Then she'd let that fearsome reality sink in for a moment and add in a calm voice, "But I'm going to save your life today." And she would mete out punishment before our father got wind of our crime.

12

We did all the things normal families do. My sisters and I were always playing outside with other kids from the neighborhood. We were rarely indoors, rarely watched television or played video games—even in the dead of winter.

Mom went all out at family cookouts, having the kids put on a dance routine or do a skit or perform in a talent show in full costume. Mom would be in the cast, too. Dad could always be talked into playing the spoons or something equally goofy. My mother always had activities planned for us. She made our Halloween costumes herself. She had our daily and weekly schedules all mapped out. During the summer, she'd come up with games and crafts for us to participate in.

It was a picture of a solid, working class, normal American family. And we really were that, too. Aside from one small problem. *Me.* I was the fly in the ointment—a clever, rambunctious, hardheaded kid who couldn't seem to take "no" for an answer, and who was always figuring out ways around anything I viewed as an obstacle. For example, when I was in eighth grade, my sixteen-year-old sister, Kristy, had her own phone line. So I drilled a hole through the wall from my bedroom into her room, ran a line along the bottom of the baseboard and tapped into her phone line so I could make secret calls from my room. Of course, I shorted something out and the entire phone system went dead and my parents had to call the phone company.

When the repairman arrived and discovered my splice job, he asked my parents, "Who did this?" I fessed up. "Well," he responded with a chuckle, "you were pretty close, kid. Just one wire off."

That's what my dad had to deal with; a kid who was constantly one wire off.

Not only did I test my parents, but I also tested the nuns at our Catholic elementary school. The sisters had a rule that you had to wear socks with your shoes. Not entirely unreasonable. Unless you were me. I didn't want to wear socks. My dad said, "You have to wear socks, it's the rule." So I cut my socks off below the ankles and wore just the tops of the socks so it would look like I had socks on. "Incorrigible," the nuns called me. "Enterprising," I responded. But, to keep the peace, I wore socks from then on. The types with the bottoms on.

The nuns also required us to wear ties. But they were running a little racket: If you forgot or lost your tie, the sisters would rent you one for a dollar a day. So I decided to cut into their business. I told my mother I had lost a tie and she bought me another one. I did this every so often, eventually amassing a little tie stash. I then rented ties to students for fifty cents a pop, undercutting the nuns by half. My mom and dad discovered my tie collection and put me out of business.

But it wasn't so much my cleverness or business acumen that got me into trouble growing up. It was my stubborn streak. My mom's family was Italian, and she had two daughters and two sisters—one of whom also had daughters. There were no sons in the entire family except for me. So, as the only boy in an Italian family, I developed a bit of an "heir apparent" attitude and, as a result, a streak of defiance. I didn't always accept it when someone told me I couldn't or shouldn't do something.

My father blamed my mother's Italian side of the family for my stubbornness. But my dad's side had its rebels, too. His British grandfather was eighty-four years old, had one eye and needed two canes to get around, but it didn't stop him from getting into a fistfight with a neighbor. When the police arrived, he threw a large, metal milk box at them through the front door. He was arrested for breach of peace. At the court hearing, the judge looked at my great-grandfather and quipped, "What am I supposed to do with this guy?" Then he released him to our custody.

After we picked him up, we held a barbeque for him. For a second-grader, having my great-grandfather tossed in the pokey for disturbing the peace and then getting feted at a family party afterward was a powerful image. If my great-granddad could stand up to authority and look like a hero, why not me?

From the time I was three years old I was constantly butting heads with my father. His punishment often involved my being sent to my room. So I would stomp into my room and slam my door behind me, muttering, "Who are they to tell me?" The last time I ever did that, I was twelve. My father said to me, "You only live in that bedroom, Bryan, but I *own* this house. That room is mine. That door is mine. Don't slam it again." Of course, I did slam it again. And he took the door off of its hinges. I lived for many years in that bedroom with a sheet hung over the doorway. It's tough to slam a sheet with any authority.

Finally, one day I'd had enough of all the restrictions and punishments, and I blurted out, "I'm running away! I can take care of myself." And I thought I could, too, because from the time I was a kid, I'd always had a job. Down at the end of our street was a small drugstore where I would spend at least half of my money on candy. In fact, the lady behind the counter had given me my very first job, picking up trash in the parking lot for a candy bar and three dollars, every other week. When I was older, I started a neighborhood landscaping business, mowing lawns for five bucks during the summer. I had fifteen accounts and was earning $60 a week. For a kid in elementary school, that was a lot of dough.

So, I had saved up some money from my landscaping business and it was time to run away from home. But I didn't go far. I tromped down the street to the Chinese restaurant and ordered a dish of every single thing I could afford on the menu. With Chinese food, you can spend $50 and have a feast fit for an emperor. I lugged my little banquet home to eat on the picnic table in the back yard. My sisters and parents happened to be in the middle of dinner, eating something like shepherd's pie, looking out the window in disbelief as I laid out my spread and chowed down, pretending not to notice them watching me. I was in heaven. That was me, running away, doing my own thing as if I could take care of myself at twelve years old. In style, too, if I wanted.

My dad wasn't impressed with my stubborn defiance. He and my mother were simply determined to make me into a man of substance.

But I was just trying to stay focused and alive.

* * *

When I was growing up, I used to take a lot of naps. My sisters would call me "grumpy." But it had nothing to do with my stubbornness or my clashes with my dad. I wasn't grumpy, I was just tired a lot—more than I should have been as a kid. I overcompensated for the constant undercurrent of fatigue by working extra hard at everything I did, whether it was running or hockey or playing with my buddies. In fact, when I was in sixth grade, I had come in second in the nation in the four-hundred meter run at the Hershey Track and Field Meet. After the meet, I wondered if I could have trained harder, because I had trained to *win*, not to come in second. But what I didn't know, what I couldn't know as a kid—what none of us could have even guessed in our wildest speculation—was that under the surface there was something fighting me. I didn't *want* to seem grumpy all the time or feel tired so often or be argumentative with my dad so much. It wasn't that at all.

It was much worse than that.

But what did we know, back then?

CHAPTER 3

Light of My Life

The grounds and buildings of Avon Old Farms School in Avon, CT looked like ancient castles with modern, cutting edge additions. In 1992, when I was sixteen, my parents sent me to the private prep school for my last two years of high-school. The feeling of unity at Avon was so familiar to my own traditions of community and family that my transition from home to boarding school was seamless. At home, I had two sisters. At Avon—an all-boys school—I had 380 brothers. We played games and sports, we studied and hung out together. It was one big family. Every morning, the students and faculty would gather in the auditorium for Morning Meeting, where the headmaster would stand center stage and announce important world events, give updates about the school community, and discuss the school agenda for the day. This was followed by faculty announcements and uplifting revelations about particular students, after which the floor was opened to students for our comments and input.

Avon gave students responsibility and a sense of freedom that was lacking at my public high school. They tied responsibility in with accountability and let every student know that they cared personally about them. They took a genuine interest in our personal and scholastic growth. It was unique, it was refreshing, it was *adult*. They encouraged us to get involved in anything that interested us academically. There were rules, of course, but the school invited open discussion about them.

Each Sunday, we would attend vespers in the chapel. Distinguished guests would come to speak, ranging from media celebrities such as Dith Pran (whose experiences were portrayed in the movie *The Killing Fields*), to elected officials, to athletes, to notable alumni. The teachers at Avon were authoritative academic educators, as well as life instructors to whom I felt I could also turn to as friends. The school's traditions and exemplary classroom teaching were top-notch. But the greatest value for me was the life lessons and positive role models.

I played hockey at Avon and made lifetime friends on the team. Our coach, a stern and highly respected leader, had a way of making even the toughest workout fun. During my junior year, we won the New England Prep School hockey championship. The following year, we were runners-up. Since we were a highly-ranked team, practices were particularly tough at Avon. Games against our rivals were never cakewalks. After games, teammates would sometimes joke that I had a yellow tinge to my eyes. I joked back that I was part wolf. I figured I was just exhausted from the grueling physical workouts.

I couldn't have been more wrong. But I didn't worry about it all that much. Love was around the corner.

* * *

After graduating from Avon Old Farms in 1994, I enrolled at the University of Connecticut. My plan at UConn was to earn a bachelor of science in sociology with a focus on criminology. As long as I can remember, I had wanted to go into federal law enforcement. My dad had worked his way up the ranks at the United States Postal Service and was now in a high level security position. As the Northeast Area Security Coordinator, he tested post office security—scaling fences, sneaking into buildings, testing and assessing security at postal facilities around the country. I had acquired his stealthy ability and developed a desire to pursue law enforcement work. He offered to help me get an internship with the U.S. Postal Inspection Service once I neared graduation from UConn.

At least that was the plan. Then reality hit.

I had obviously been having too much fun at UConn, because by the end of my first semester, my grades were in the toilet. At the rate I was going, there was no way I would get an internship with the Postal Inspection Service. Heck, I wouldn't even be able to show my face in the local post office to buy a stamp. Federal law enforcement? Ha! I'd be lucky to get a job as a security guard down at the mall. My dad was going to flat *kill me*.

And then, my penchant for stubbornly figuring my way around obstacles kicked into gear. During my lip-biting drive home for Christmas break, I came up with a simple, yet brilliant, plan to get my rear out of a sling with my dad: join the U.S. Marines. He couldn't kill me if I was in Marine Corps boot camp when he got my transcripts in the mail. A sense of relief came over me at my cleverness. I pulled a U-turn, headed for the nearest recruitment office and signed up.

Then I drove home to deliver the news.

My dad and mom went speechless with anger when I explained to them that I was now a U.S. Marine. Before my dad could launch into one of his angry tirades and send me to my door-less bedroom, and while he calmed himself down enough to mete out my punishment, I said, "Wait, Dad—hear me out on this. I have a plan. This will be a great opportunity to get some discipline into me and develop a military background, so when I go back to school and get my degree in criminology, I'll be an ideal candidate for federal law enforcement."

As I was laying out my plan, my father was looking at me as if I were singing a warbly rendition of "Kumbaya" while puffing a doobie on the hood of his car. I'd never seen neck veins so big and blue. When I finished, he shook his head in disbelief and sputtered, "Well . . . whatever I was going to do to you is *nothing* compared to what they're gonna do to you in boot camp."

"Dad," I smiled as if he were the son and I was the dad, patiently explaining how life works, "I am *extremely* physically fit. I can handle it."

By then, my mom had slumped down to the couch like a sack of potatoes, probably replaying the family line in her mind, trying to figure out the source of my sudden lack of good sense.

I continued, needlessly running down my athletic resume to my dad. "I played *varsity hockey* at Avon, Dad. How hard can boot camp be?"

"Bryan," he deadpanned, "that was *high school*."

"But I was ranked *second in the nation* in the four-hundred meter run at Hershey!"

"You were *twelve!*"

"Dad," I pressed on, "I have never scored less than perfect on any physical fitness test—*ever*. What's a few jumping jacks and early morning jogs to a machine like me? Boot camp will be a breeze. You'll see."

That brought a chuckle. He walked away, shaking his head. There was no punishment.

Until I got to boot camp.

He was right. I struggled big time in boot camp at Parris Island. True, I was a gifted athlete and could handle a lot of the physical regimen, but I was still a teenager, and was still resisting the "obey or else" mentality and discipline of military life. As the only boy growing up in an Italian family, I had been favored a bit by family members, and had become a stubborn little cuss who had no problem bucking my dad's strictness. But he was nothing compared to foam-mouthed, raging Marine drill instructors, or DIs, with no sense of humor who constantly shouted and waved their arms like they were addressing a field full of mutes. *Nothing* was reasonable to the DIs. They wanted *nothing* to come out of your mouth except "SIR, *YES SIR!*" They would not tolerate an ounce of stubbornness from the recruits.

My dad must have enjoyed every one of my ninety painful days at Parris Island. My scheme to avoid punishment for my bad grades at UConn by joining the Marines seemed to be backfiring. That is, until Tim Shields, my closest friend in boot camp, gave me some advice that would echo far into my future. One day at the end of a particularly grueling week of training, when I was feeling I couldn't take much more, Tim said to me, "It's all a game, Bryan. Don't let them break you. If you break, *you lose.*"

And suddenly, everything clicked: Self discipline was at the core of all we do in life, and it's a *choice*—one that starts in the mind. The solution, then, was the power of *thought*; in particular, to disciplining and controlling the choices we have to make daily to get through life. Those three months in boot camp were the genesis of my understanding that the course of one's life—with all of its accomplishments, successes and even its failures—is rooted in every decision we choose to make along the way. Each choice is a building block in the construction of our future. The more well-thought-out our decisions, the more solid and unshakable our life. It's all in our mental attitude.

Right then and there, as a teenager in the U.S. Marine Corps, I became determined to change my thinking and my mindset about how I looked at life, and to learn to positively influence my course simply by changing my way of thinking.

After three months of boot camp, I went into the Marine Corps Reserves, and re-enrolled in UConn on the GI Bill. To my parents' surprise, my plan was working—due in no small measure to my attitude change.

And my timing was perfect. I was about to meet a girl.

* * *

In the fall of 1995, I started my second semester at UConn. Boot camp was behind me and I was a jarhead reservist in the Corps. I got settled into my second-floor dorm room and met some of my neighbors and classmates. One neighbor who stood out lived on the floor above me. Her name was Lia. A petite, breathtaking, soft-spoken beauty of Italian descent, just one year younger than me. So smart and beautiful she could have chosen to become anything from a rocket scientist to a featured TV actress. To say I fell hard would be trivial. She melted me.

I couldn't let her know that, of course, because she was in the last stages of an up-and-down relationship with her high-school boyfriend. So I contented myself to seeing her whenever I could, mostly through friends we had in common, or classes we had together. We became friendly. There was *chemistry*. I enjoyed every second I was around her.

The following semester, in 1996, Lia saw the light and ended her relationship with the high-school sweetheart. We went out on a couple of dates, but there was nothing official between us. Then, one afternoon while hanging out in my dorm room together, I was doing all I could to resist the urge to kiss her. So I kissed her. It was sparks from the get-go. I was the fun-loving jarhead and she, the dark-eyed beauty. Soon, we began officially dating.

Amazing how a pretty, Italian girl can inspire a young Marine to settle down.

My parents took to Lia immediately, convinced I had won the lottery. That was an understatement. In fact, Lia was so nice that the running joke about her was that she was born at Disney World.

In academics, Lia was a godsend to me. During an Italian literature class we had together, for example, I didn't always have time to read the book. (Okay, I didn't *take* the time to read the book; I still had that stubborn streak to work out of me, a trait that made her want to strangle me sometimes.) On our way to class, I would say to her, "Tell me what we read last night." And she would give me the *Reader's Digest* rundown of what we were supposed to have read for class—which, of course, she had thoroughly read and I hadn't even touched. The professor would give a test on the material, which included writing a personal interpretation of the book. I would write my interpretation based on the synopsis Lia had given me about the material. By some miracle, I seemed to always get a higher test score than she did.

"How could you get a higher grade than me when you didn't even read the book?!" she would blurt out, dumbfounded.

But in the end, the professor figured me out and gave me a final grade lower than Lia's. I had the gall to go to him and ask, "How did this happen, that I got good test scores during the semester but got a lower final grade?"

He gave me a look like Robert DeNiro in *Goodfellas*, and answered, "You know, Bryan. *You know.*"

Yeah. I did know. I dodged another bullet. Something I would find myself doing a lot in my twenties.

* * *

In the summer of 1997, I was with my Marine unit at Twentynine Palms, California, for desert training. It was the end of June. The temperature was touching 110 degrees at midday and my skin had become so itchy I was scratching until I bled. I thought I was going insane. I didn't know what was causing it. All I knew was that the itching, the heat and the sand were all driving me crazy. So I went to the medic and was told that I was probably having an allergic reaction to something in the desert. He told me to take Benadryl. Problem was, Benadryl makes you drowsy and I was in Motor Transport, driving Hummers and five-ton trucks. Once they put me on Benadryl, I was no longer allowed to drive. So I lay in a large, hot tent, sweating and itching, hot as hell, and going nuts in the desert.

But the strange itching continued after the training ended and I'd returned to Connecticut. Some nights, I would lay in bed in my shoebox dorm room so itchy that I would scratch all night. Obviously, something wasn't right. No one seemed to be able to tell me why I was itching so badly. Something far more complicated than mere allergies was going on inside of me. Lia convinced me to go to the campus infirmary. When we arrived, I heard familiar words that made no sense and I didn't want to hear. "Bryan," she said, "your eyes look yellowish." *Who cares about my eyes*, I thought, *I'm bleeding from scratching so much!* I was convinced I was going out of my mind.

When I was finally taken into the exam room, the doctor looked at my skin and told me that I was suffering a bad reaction to soap or laundry detergent. Or that I just had plain dry skin. They gave me some lotion and told me to change the soap and detergent I was using, and sent me home. To me, that seemed too easy of a fix after having scratched my skin to bloody ribbons. After a few days, though, I felt okay.

But something was nagging at me. Something inside me.

Things went from bad to worse. During a Marine training exercise in the fall of 1997, I tore my ACL and was told I would have to go in for knee surgery. I would be on crutches for a couple of months. But in order to have the surgery and recuperate properly and not miss a semester in college, I would have to transfer from UConn to Southern Connecticut State University, which was closer to my home.

I had little choice. I made the move. Lia stayed at UConn and visited each week. I started school at Southern and settled into my new routine, healing up and working toward my degree. Later that year, I was thrilled to learn that I had been accepted for a six-month internship with the U.S. Postal Inspection Service. Although I was still experiencing occasional pain and discomfort from the surgery, and the weird itching problem had returned, I was elated. Life couldn't be better.

But the hammer was about to drop.

CHAPTER

Yesterday Forever

How great it is that we live in a country at a time when we have the ability and the opportunity to live the life we choose, and to succeed if we really want to. We're not guaranteed happiness, but we are guaranteed the right to pursue it. Shame on us if we don't take advantage of that—it's free. This point was always reinforced in our home when I was a kid. It was an American freedom my father was proud to participate in. He wanted his children to know that we live in a great place where we could be who we wanted to be and do what we wanted to do. We had been given the opportunities. All we had to do was decide what we wanted; and whatever that was, it was ours to pursue.

* * *

By spring of 1998, I had been in the Marine Corps Reserves for four years. Other than a torn ligament in my knee the previous year, I was in better physical condition than ever. I had transferred to Southern Connecticut State University, well on my way to earning my degree. And I was dating the girl of my dreams. Summer was in the air. Aerosmith's "Don't Want to Miss a Thing" was in heavy airplay, along with Natalie Imbruglia's "Torn" and Green Day's "Time of Your Life." It sure was the time of my life. Even though I was twenty-two, in many ways I was still a kid. But the relative ease of my life was about to change. Hard and fast.

One beautiful Thursday in April of 1998, I went to visit Lia at UConn. I had a couple of beers—and almost immediately fell violently ill. I became disoriented and began vomiting excessively, as if I were heavily intoxicated. I was so sick that my urine was the color of tea and I was throwing up bile. It made no sense. I went to bed that night and couldn't get up until the following Saturday evening, and I was still nauseous and dehydrated.

Lia's roommate, a nursing student, took one look at me and said urgently, "Something is *really* wrong with you, Bryan. You need to get to a doctor."

But my younger sister, Amy, was at UConn for the weekend and she and her friends were on their way over to visit us. So I dragged myself out of bed and put on my game face, because I didn't want Amy to be concerned about how sick I was. But I couldn't protect her for long. Everyone would find out soon enough.

It was a Donahue thing, a Marine thing, to ignore pain. In the Marine Corps, they teach you that pain is weakness leaving the body. More than ever, I needed to maintain that attitude. *It'll go away. Tough it out. Don't be a wimp. Don't complain. Don't be grumpy. A quitter never wins and a winner never quits.* So I toughed it out that weekend at UConn and went home on Sunday. But I knew there was something seriously wrong inside of me.

A few weeks later, on June 9, it happened again. As I was getting ready to leave for class, I experienced an intense pain in my right side. The night before, I'd eaten at a seafood restaurant and thought maybe I'd had too much fried food. The next morning, the pain began as a bad cramp and became so unbearable that I began to sweat through my clothes and was vomiting violently.

"I'm going to take you to the doctor," my mother said anxiously. "Just let me get changed first."

"I can't wait, Mom," I groaned, in too much pain to wait. "I have to go *now*."

I drove to my doctor in Hamden. His preliminary evaluation confirmed jaundice and gastroenteritis. He sent me immediately to the hospital, where several tests were run. My blood platelet count was abnormally low. The diagnosis was "gallstones." They ordered surgery and removed my gallbladder.

That was my first experience with any kind of serious internal health issue. I was relieved when it was behind me, because I had been accepted to the internship program with the U.S. Postal Inspection Service and was eager to get a first real taste of my federal law enforcement career.

On June 16, after a week of recovery and feeling back to my invincible self, I went in for my post-op checkup. After some poking and prodding, the doctor instructed me to follow-up with his professor, a "preeminent specialist" named Marshall Kaplan, at Tufts New England Medical Center in Boston. Not being medically savvy at the time, I didn't inquire as to why I had to drive all the way to a prestigious medical clinic in Massachusetts—two hours away in the best of traffic—for a post-op checkup with a specialist. I was miffed at the inconvenience. Neither U.S. Marines nor college students like to spend more than drive-by time anywhere near hospitals.

At Tufts, Dr. Kaplan examined me, made a few odd faces, and peered intently at the lab work in my file. He was particularly interested in the results of my gallbladder operation and a complex lab workup done on me called an "ERCP" (endoscopic retrograde cholangio pancreatography). The ERCP, he explained, diagnoses problems and diseases related to the liver, including gallstones, blockage of the bile duct, yellowing of the skin and eyes, darkening of the urine, undiagnosed upper abdominal pain, fatigue, itching, night sweats, buildup of fluid in the stomach, chills, fever, etc. I already knew about those symptoms; I'd been experiencing every one of them with increasing intensity over the years.[1] The ERCP examination had been no fun, either. It involved inserting an endoscope down my throat, then a thin tube inserted through the endoscope all the way through the duodenum to my main bile duct.

But that procedure, the X-rays, and the sore throat it caused me would prove to be the least of my problems.

Still musing over the paperwork, Dr. Kaplan announced, "About three to six months."

I groaned. "I really don't want to drive all the way back here in three months—or six months, doc," I complained. "That's two whole hours—*each way*."

Once was plenty of needless driving for me. I stood and started buttoning my shirt.

Kaplan sat down in the chair in front of me and peered at me silently. "My God," he stated quietly after an uneasy moment. "You don't know, do you?"

"Know what?" I asked. The solemn look on his face and his hesitation before he answered told me to sit back down. I sat. "*What* don't I know, doc?"

"You only have maybe three to six months . . . *to live.*"

Talk about being hit in the chest with a sledgehammer. I don't remember what else the doctor said that day. I don't remember driving back to Connecticut. I don't remember stopping at any of the three toll booths on my way home. I don't even remember driving to Lia's apartment to give her the news. It was like my car was on autopilot and I was the lone passenger as we drifted vaguely in the direction of home.

---

1. For sources for this chapter, see: "Primary Sclerosing Cholangitis" study by Marshall M. Kaplan, M.D., February 6, 1998; and a *New England Journal of Medicine*, April 6, 1995, article titled "Medical Progress: Primary Sclerosing Cholangitis."

I felt as healthy as a bull. I was a U.S. Marine. I was in college. I had an incredible girlfriend. I was dying.

I wished it was yesterday, forever.

The course of your life changes in a blink when you're told you are about to die. Before I knew that the pain I'd been experiencing was being caused by a rare killer, I had run some worst case scenarios in my mind. *I might have to miss the hockey game on Saturday . . . When am I going to study for that poli-sci test?* Not once ever did I think, *Wonder when I'll have time to plan my funeral?* Nobody does that. Unless they know they're dying.

The day before I was diagnosed, I thought I knew everything there was to know. I was young. I hadn't thought much about dreams or long term plans—my future was as far away as east is from west. Now, I'd never have a chance to fulfill anything, much less any of my dreams. I had always known, like most young people, that I wanted to be successful at *something*, but I figured I had all the time in the world to sort that all out. Not anymore. I had to get serious, quick.

Six months is a short time to plan a life's legacy.

* * *

I was diagnosed with a rare liver disease called primary sclerosing cholangitis ("PSC"), a progressive hardening and scaring of the bile ducts that filter toxins out of the body.[2] The liver is the largest single organ in the body and performs the most functions. It helps digest food, clears wastes from the blood, makes proteins that help blood to clot, stores glycogen

---

2.   The body rids itself of poisons by casting them off in the bile.

for energy, produces essential proteins, stores vitamins, breaks down poisons, and works with the body's immune system.

If you imagine the bile duct system as a tree, the common bile duct is the trunk and the further up the tree you go, the smaller the duct branches become. Technology can see these smaller branches, but can't physically get into them to unblock them. When bile is unable to drain properly through the ducts, it accumulates in the liver, and the ducts gradually become clogged, which allows toxins to shut down healthy liver tissue. Eventually, so much bile is accumulated that it seeps into the bloodstream and begins a whole new level of destruction throughout the body.

When the liver is badly damaged, it can't re-grow enough tissue to heal itself—and you can no more live without a liver than you can without a heart. Actually, you can live without a heart if you have a mechanical pump . . . but there are no mechanical liver replacements. You do not live without a liver. *Period.*

The statistics of the disease were terrifying. PSC progresses silently, but relentlessly. In Stage IV, the one I was in, PSC causes cirrhosis (basically, the destruction of the small bile ducts). Most of the damage is too small to be visualized radiologically and brings with it an increased risk of bile duct cancer.[3] Seventy percent of those who have PSC are males; nearly half are under forty-five years old at the time of diagnosis (the average age at diagnosis is thirty-nine—I was a pup in comparison). A vast majority of patients have no symptoms before diagnosis. Yet, some patients, while asymptomatic, are surprisingly advanced in the disease. In fact, patients who are symptomatic at diagnosis tend to live a shorter time than those who have no symptoms—and the survival rate of the ones with symptoms is

---

3.   In fact, PSC is often difficult to distinguish from bile duct cancer.

significantly shorter, with median survival only nine to twelve years from diagnosis.

There are only around 30,000 people in the America who have PSC. To describe a disease that afflicts one out of every ten thousand people as "rare" would be an understatement. You'd have better odds of throwing a 7 seven times in a row on seven consecutive days at the tables in Vegas than being diagnosed with PSC. And there is no proven therapy, effective drugs, treatment, or cure for the disease.

I was deep in it.

* * *

"You probably had PSC as early as ninth grade," Dr. Kaplan told me.

Everything—my entire life—suddenly all made sense. I'd had symptoms all along that I didn't tell anybody about—that I'd had no clue that even *were* symptoms. I had made light of my odd ailments because I didn't know what was going on inside me. I never went to the doctor for any of it. I was tired a lot, always fatigued and taking naps. In fact, my dad would get on me for sleeping so much, and my sisters and friends constantly made a thing of it. I just thought I was a lazy kid. I didn't know—none of us knew. The jaundice in my eyes I would brush off because what high-schooler would even know what something like that was all about? You just accept those kinds of things in your friends, like you accept a crooked nose, or a funny walk, or goofy laugh.

But my symptoms were all there. I just explained them as—

Just recovering from a torn ACL.

Just a case of gallstones.

Just tired a lot from all the sports.

Just overcompensating by becoming a super athlete to stay on my game.

Just a grumpy kid.

Even in college, if I had only two beers, the next morning I'd have yellow eyes and be vomiting fluorescent green bile. I thought it was just the Incredible Hulk of hangovers. "Lightweight," the guys probably chuckled behind my back.

I'd take that diagnosis any day over what was really going on.

As a young man barely launching out into life, it was a frightening challenge to try to maintain an optimistic attitude while facing a life or death battle. Not to mention remaining hopeful that a cure might soon be found, and that I might actually have a shot at living a long and enjoyable life.

But to put things in perspective, in February of 1999, just eight months after I was diagnosed, Super Bowl-winning running back Walter Payton—one of the top five-ranked football players in the history of the sport—was diagnosed with the same disease. He was dead by that Thanksgiving.

If this disease could put a superman like Walter Payton in the grave in just months . . . what chance did I have?

It takes a lot to make a Marine cry. All I could think about was the wonderful life I'd had on this amazing planet. I was going to miss it. Best twenty-two years a man could ever have. What I faced next was the hardest thing I'd ever done in my life: telling my family and friends. I cried like a baby because I didn't want to see them sad. And, I was scared. Not so much because I was dying . . . but because I hadn't yet really lived.

* * *

My parents were devastated. They never dreamed I was *that* sick. Nobody in my family even knew this disease existed.

After the initial impact of learning what I was dealing with, and knowing that the statistics on PSC indicated that I didn't have much time to live, I decided to carry through with my internship with the U.S. Postal Inspection Service. It was a phenomenal experience, made all the more bittersweet by the fact that I was dying. I loved the people. I loved the work. I loved the challenges and the learning.

But I would not be working in law enforcement, federal or otherwise. Because there came a point when I could no longer handle the physical regimen I was undergoing in so many areas of my life. The physicality of law enforcement, the physical exertion of being a Marine, the physical requirements of my sports activities. With the disease ravaging my body, it all became too much. Mentally, I felt like I could do it all, but when the results of my medical exams came in . . . well, reality can be a hard slap. The illness was simply keeping me from doing the physical parts of all of the work I had come to love.

My body was finally saying, *Enough*. It's time to die.

Things began a rapid deterioration as the silent progression stage of the disease ended, and it really started showing its fangs.

On August 8, 1999, I was again rushed to the emergency room.

By fall of 1999, when I was in my last semester of college, infections in my liver and all of the vicious symptoms of PSC were in full-throated roar throughout my body. During the afternoon of September 13, I was sitting on my parents' back deck in pain, fatigued from vomiting, scratching my legs raw, and glowing yellow as a ghost from jaundice. When my mom got home, she immediately rushed me to St. Raphael Hospital. I was there for five days, sleeping on ice blankets to keep the fever down. Doctors were at a loss as to what to do. They put me on intravenous antibiotics. When my temperature finally came down, they released me, though I was still in great pain. Of course, I would never admit how bad it was. But a parent knows.

It was time to take stronger measures. I was going downhill faster than I could continue to fake. Later that afternoon, my parents went back to the hospital and retrieved all my medical records. That evening, several friends and family members arrived to visit me. Lia never left my side. My longtime friend Muchie showed up. He and I used to play hockey together, traveling many weekends in pursuit of the sport we loved. We looked so much alike that Muchie could have been the brother I never had. I wondered if my mom would be able to bear looking at him after I died.

While I was fading away that evening, my parents were on the phone, frantic to get me into a different hospital, one that was better equipped to deal with what I was suffering from. They settled on Tufts New England Medical Center, where Dr. Kaplan practiced. I was barely able to sit up on the bed to put on my shoes for the long drive to Boston. Muchie grabbed my shoes and began helping me into them. My mother was watching from the doorway as Muchie kneeled down to tie my laces. Tears were streaming silently down his cheeks. My mother turned and quickly left the room.

I was in severe pain lying on the back seat during the long, silent drive to Boston's Chinatown, where Tufts was located. Other than coping with my pain and discomfort, all I'd had to do was take my medication, follow the plan, and report to the hospital. The support team I had around me was incredible; my parents and Lia took charge of all the other things—insurance forms, costs, transportation. They did all they could to reduce my stress so I could deal with the physical and emotional strain.

We arrived in Boston just before midnight. It was a Saturday. In September. In Boston, a major college town. The city was teeming with parents and college students returning to school for the fall semester. Hotels were booked solid; none had vacancies. I was in severe pain. And then we got lost. It was a powder keg in the car. After a few frantic, fearful minutes, we found the hospital and went straight to the emergency room. Doctors inserted a stent and fought to get my symptoms under control.

The hospital offered my parents and Lia a very small room to stay in, one used by doctors and residents. It had a Murphy bed, a recliner and little else. Dr. Kaplan explained the grim reality of what I was facing. A liver transplant might have been an option, he said, but they weren't doing live donor liver transplants for victims of PSC.

My body may have been dying, but my mind and my spirit were alive and well. I did all I could to kick my mental attitude into high gear . . . while preparing for the worst.

* * *

Figuring out ways to buck the system when I was a kid had helped me more than any of us had ever realized it could, because my inherent stubbornness caused me to not necessarily accept things at face value. When someone tells you that you're going to die, for example, it's reassuring to be able to respond, "No, I'm not"—and *mean it*. Now, all that stubbornness would be put to its ultimate test. Death wanted me. I wanted life.

Winning this battle would require a completely different way of thinking than I was accustomed to. At the very least, I would need a mindset that would transform my ebbing life from simply breathing, while waiting for death to take me or a cure to be discovered, to living a fulfilling life—with no regrets, no matter how few months I had left to live. Yet, for a guy in his early twenties, the challenge of transitioning to the mindset of a healthy life and choosing an attitude of gratefulness while a disease has its claws in you and is dragging you toward the grave . . . was daunting. But I was determined to choose to see my bad days as good days, and my okay days as great ones. Because I didn't have many of either remaining.

I may have been at the mercy of the illness, but emotionally and mentally, *I* was in charge. I alone would decide my attitude about the journey ahead. And it would be a journey that would teach me to literally stop and smell the roses along the path of this incredible gift called "life" that each of us are privileged to experience.

* * *

I was in the hospital for twenty-two days. They sent me home with a PICC line inserted in the bend of my elbow joint that went into a vein in my armpit and into my heart. I gave myself antibiotics through the line four times a day for nearly three weeks. I had in-home care so I wouldn't have to be in Boston for awhile.

My parents and I argued about who they were going to tell about my condition and how much they would reveal. I made a decision not to let my little sister Amy know the extent of what I was dealing with, because she was the youngest. It was easy to hide my condition from her, because she was away at college, in Providence. I didn't want people to know how sick I was, because I didn't want to be treated differently. I didn't want them worrying or feeling bad for me. Too much sympathy could lead to too much dwelling on the illness, and I didn't want to give PSC that kind of power. But my older sister Kristy knew what was happening, because she had an apartment nearby and was around home more often.

In the meantime, I continued to fight to stay in school, even though I'd missed three weeks of my last semester. The university advised me to withdraw and return in the spring. I stubbornly refused. My academic advisor was solidly in my corner. My parents contacted school officials and pressed my case. The university relented and agreed to allow me to continue working to finish my degree. I went to school every day between treatments, wearing long-sleeved shirts and taping the PICC line to my arm so nobody would see it. The simple joy of strolling across campus was a painful struggle. I would have to rest halfway because I was breathing so hard from mere walking. Still, I was fighting a good battle. I'd managed to make up all the schoolwork I'd missed.

Then, on September 18, 1999, Dr. Kaplan called to inform me that, by all criteria, the disease was most likely too advanced to respond to further medical treatment. He began a liver transplantation evaluation. Ten days later, the Transplant Evaluation Committee at Tufts New England Medical Center put me on the list for a liver transplant. Even so, the waiting list for liver transplants was many years long. And even being on the donor list was no guarantee, because the way the list works, the longer you're on it, the farther down from the top you tend to wind up as new, more urgent and immediately life-threatening cases enter the system.

The best we could hope for was an experimental treatment program Dr. Kaplan ran that he said might buy me some time while specialists continued to search for a cure. He had been working with a doctor in Chicago and one in England (they were world-renowned physicians for their research on PSC). The medication was originally made to dissolve gallstones in women. Medical researchers observed that the drug also thinned out liver bile, enabling it to flow more readily through the tiny, twisted bile ducts. This allowed use of the drug to slow the advance of PSC while a cure was sought.

I put my life in Dr. Kaplan's hands.

The next blow was my military status, I was given a medical discharge from the Marine Corps under "honorable" conditions. But it didn't feel honorable. A Marine would rather face bullets than be drummed out of the Corps—for any reason.

My father's words that day reminded me of those of my friend Tim Shields when I was in boot camp. "Attitude is everything in life," my dad told me. "And attitude is a choice you have to make. So there's really only one answer here, Bryan. *Win.*"

My mom added, "In life, you have to pick your battles. There are battles to walk away from because they're just not that important in the overall picture. But this is a battle you must *win*, Bryan. This one *you fight.*"

My parents were right. My choice was simple. Win. *Period.*

In January 2000, I graduated from Southern Connecticut State University, earning a bachelor of science degree in sociology with a focus in criminology. Though I had at last accomplished one major goal in life, it was not the happy occasion it should have been. After all, how do you face living while actively dying?

* * *

By February of 2000, it was time to sit down and write a letter. After I wrote it, I put it in a sealed envelope and gave it to my father. I told him I wanted it back when I was better.

And if I never got better, then upon my death, he was to share it with all the family members, including wives, husbands and children . . .

Hi, everyone.

Chances are that if you're reading this letter, I am no longer with you. You all mean the world to me. I truly cannot think of any better people in the world and I am glad that I am a part of your lives, just as you all are a part of mine.

Although we have argued and fought with each other at times, I never doubted your love. I just hope that you all can say the same of me.

As I am writing this letter, I think of the past and those great memories and I pray for a positive future. My eyes are full of tears, but not because I am feeling sorry for myself or afraid of the future. It is because I want to stay here with all of you. Please don't dwell over the fact that I was sick, but celebrate my life. I do not want this to be a sad time for all of you. Please share with each other your memories of our good times.

If there is one thing that I ask of you all, it is not to stall your lives, go on and live them to the fullest. You all have too much good in your hearts, you need to share it. Never be afraid or feel alone; I will always be by your sides. If it is possible, I will let you know that I am alright.

Although this letter actually took one hour to write, it really took me a year and a half. I want to thank all of you for being such a great family and the best friends imaginable. Being able to be a part of your lives completed my life.

Don't be afraid or sad; be happy and secure, because I will never leave you.

I love all of you forever,
Bryan

As positive as I could often pump myself up to feel, and as strong and encouraging as my family and friends were around me, the wolf was always at the door, and the anguish of the conflicting emotions crashing within me would shove aside my determined stoicism. And so I readied my affairs.[4]

---

4. My family knows this letter exists, but until this book was published, they had never read it.

CHAPTER 5

Stand by Your Man

We will either find a way, or make one.

—Hannibal (247–182 B.C.),
Carthaginian General, Statesman

The bright spot in all I was going through was Lia. We had met in 1995 and started dating in 1996. In 1998, I was diagnosed with PSC, and here it was, the new millennium, and she was still with me. Not many twenty-year-old college students—even if they were in love—would stay in a relationship with someone who had a terminal illness. Yet, during my intensifying ordeal, Lia never complained, never wavered; her love never deserted me. Even when I was told that having children was not in my future, she stood by me. Her heart and positive energy knew no bounds. Her steadfast faithfulness and unshakable love kept my spirit ablaze with desire to *live*.

Lia's parents, George and Fran Dickerson, lived in Newtown, Connecticut. George was a retired police officer—though, if you encountered him out of uniform on the street, you'd never guess he was a cop. George was so nice as a peace officer that he would make friends with strangers, as opposed to eyeing them with suspicion. Even within the police force itself, he was averse to the confrontation aspects of law enforcement. For example, when officers broke a departmental regulation, they were often reprimanded by being assigned jail duty, where the routine was mundane and the action virtually nonexistent. But George *volunteered* for jailer duty—he enjoyed it. "It's air conditioned in the summer," he would explain, "and heated in the winter. I don't have to wrestle anyone down. I don't have to chase anyone around. And my superiors can't bust me down to the jail if I mess up, because I'm already working in the jail." He was just a nice, easygoing guy with a heart of gold. Same with Lia's mother.

George had recently retired, so he began spending a lot of time at my house. George was the canary in the coal mine of my disease. His barometer for telling how sick I was feeling on any given day was to give me a dose of ribbing. He would dole out little verbal jabs, and if I didn't respond, he would know I wasn't feeling well. But if I fired back, he got excited because that meant I at least felt well enough to spar with him. As he would get ready to go back home each day after visiting me, George would grab me in a headlock and plop a big sloppy wet kiss on my bald head. That drove me nuts. Sometimes I'd have to run out to the car and lock myself in just to get away from his goobery wet ones. And then Lia would trot out to the car and open the door and he'd climb in and plant his sloppy smackers on my head. I was constantly mopping my head down when George was around. What sane man wouldn't want to be part of a family like that? Even my sisters got along with Lia like they were all best friends.

After Lia and I graduated from college, I landed a job as an insurance claims adjuster and was living at home. Lia had moved back in with her parents, too. We were both itching to move out. Nothing to do with our parents, of course; it was just, who wants to leave the liberty of four years at college and then turn around and move back in with Mom and Dad?

By 2001, because of my disease, Lia had endured many difficult situations right along with my family and me. Her capacity to love was beyond description. As tenuous as it might have sounded, I decided to ask her to marry me. I began saving every spare penny to buy Lia a ring, and I came up with a plan to ask her to become my wife. My brother-in-law and longtime friend Jeff Agli and I went to Hamden (where I had grown up) to a mountain called Sleeping Giant, to locate the perfect spot where I could propose to Lia. We cased the surrounding area and found a place for Jeff to hide and secretly video the moment. Now all I had to do was buy the ring.

When I finally saved up enough money, one day I told Lia I was taking a day off of work to go fishing.

She shot me a funny look. "With who?"

"Alone," I fibbed.

She studied me a moment. "What guy does that?" she responded suspiciously. "Go fishing all alone?"

"I like fishing," I countered defensively.

I could almost hear her mind churning, convinced she was thinking something like, *Why wouldn't he ask Muchie or somebody to go with him?*

So I went fishing for a ring and picked out a nice solitaire diamond.

When I saw her that evening, she looked me up and down for a second and asked, "Why don't you have a sunburn if you were out in the sun, fishing all day?"

"I used sun block," I lied.

"Uh-huh," she deadpanned. "You *never* use sun block."

"Well, uh, that's probably why I didn't get burned this time," I said, then threw in quickly, "So, how'd your day go?"

Wrong question! She proceeded to tell me all about our friend Liz, who'd just become engaged and had gotten a ring with three diamonds in it. Lia was gushing on about how three diamonds were the best, three diamonds were amazing, three diamonds could cure world hunger. And all I could afford was a solitaire. So I countered that a solitaire was so much better than three diamonds, it doesn't get upstaged by two others hogging the limelight. It was the all-time classic look—arguments that no single guy ever even gets involved in.

And right in the middle of my energetic defense of the solitaire, Lia said, "Oh yeah . . . yeah, you're right, Bryan. Solitaires *are* **very** nice."

And I suddenly realized that I had been pressing my case a bit too energetically—on a topic guys don't usually get defensive about. I hoped I hadn't tipped my hand. This business of proposing was like sitting in a rocking chair in a roomful of long-tail cats.

My next-to-the-last task was to ask Lia's father for permission to marry her. I was worried about George because he was an ebullient fellow and might inadvertently spill the beans to Lia before I would even get a chance to ask her. I would have to do some fancy footwork to make sure Lia didn't get wind of my plan—not only because of the challenge of making sure her dad kept a lid on it, but also because Lia was an extremely smart and observant woman who was working on a graduate degree in psychology. I had my work cut out for me. And it was about to get even trickier: the day I chose as the day I would propose on the mountaintop, Jeff had become unavailable to hide in advance and video the scene. I would have to keep the schedule real tight, to leave little time for George to sit with the information. Because it would eat at him like Chinese water torture and he'd run screaming to tell the nearest person the good news.

Finally, the day arrived. I went to Lia's house and asked George permission to marry his daughter.

"Yes!" he beamed. "You have my permission!"

There would have been no way George could hold the excitement in for days without having to tell the world. That assessment, however, would turn out to be far too generous.

"No one knows about this," I cautioned him sternly. "So please keep it a secret, because *no one knows*. Okay, George?"

He assured me his lips were sealed like a pharaoh's tomb. As we were walking up the stairs from the basement, we heard Lia at the front door. As we stood to go upstairs, I quickly reminded George, "Remember, don't say a word. No one else knows."

"But I'll tell her mom, though, right?" he asked.

"No—don't tell anybody. Not yet. I have to ask her first—and she has to say yes."

George and I entered the family room and Lia walked in. As I approached her and hugged her, George made a surreptitious gesture to Lia's mom like he was slipping a ring on his own finger, motioning that I had bought Lia a ring and was going to ask her to marry me! We'd barely gotten out of the basement and he was already telling someone! *Oh, great!* I thought, *the same half hour I get his permission and ask him to keep his trap shut, he's already blabbing the secret!*

Lia and I loved to go hiking. But PSC and the treatments made me fatigue easily, so I wasn't doing as much hiking and biking as I used to. So she was pleasantly surprised when I asked her if she wanted to go for a sunset hike.

When we arrived at the Sleeping Giant, the setting sun was splashing a vibrant bouquet of color across the valley below. I got down on one knee. Lia thought I was tying my shoelace. I pulled out the ring. As it began to dawn on her that I was asking her to marry me, we both started shaking. She said *yes* and I slipped the ring on her finger. I was so happy I don't even remember us going back down the mountain trail.

"You picked such a beautiful spot," she said breathlessly, taking in the panorama as we walked hand in hand.

"That's because if you would have said no," I chuckled, "I was going to push you over the edge."

Lia and I went to my house and shared the news with my parents. By the time we got to Lia's house later that night to make the announcement, there were already messages on their phone machine from George's friends congratulating him. The rascal had told everyone!

Lia planned the ceremony. Our wedding song wasn't what you would call traditional, but it foretold the feelings that would continually blossom in my heart for her during the grueling experience that lay ahead: "What a Wonderful World," by Louis Armstrong.[5]

For our honeymoon, we decided to go to Tortola, British Virgin Islands. We asked Dr. Kaplan about potential health risks I should be aware of during the trip. As he gave the question some thought, I encouraged him not to hold back. "Whatever I should watch out for, doc, I'll do exactly as you say. I don't want to make my health any worse than it already is."

"Well," he began solemnly, "Yes. There is one thing that would make things even worse."

"Ok." I braced myself. "What is it?"

"Sharks," he deadpanned. "Watch out for sharks."

---

5. Written by Bob Thiele (as George Douglas) and George David Weiss. First performed by Louis Armstrong.

CHAPTER 6

Every Day
above Ground

Now that Dr. Kaplan was at work buying me some time with the ERCP procedures,[6] I could focus on some normal things. Like personal growth.

There were areas in my personality that needed attention. One of them was my tendency to become impatient with people whom I felt were pestering me about how I was feeling. I didn't want to discuss my "condition," didn't want to dwell on it, didn't want my circumstance to be a topic of endless worry and discussion and speculation. The way I dealt with comments from people who thought I wasn't looking well was to brusquely tell them I felt fine and then admonish them not to ask me anymore.

My mother would say, "How are you feeling, honey?"

"I feel fine," I would answer.

"No, you don't—not really," she'd respond, shaking her head in worry.

"Do you not *want* me to feel good?" I would snap back impatiently, hoping she would get the hint and stop dwelling on it.

"That's the last thing I would ever want, Bryan," she would answer with a hurt expression.

I didn't want to be curt or short or rude with anyone. Yet, there I was, doing exactly that to my own mom. What I had to overcome was my tendency to feel pestered. I went around thinking, *You asked, I answered, now drop it and move on.* That attitude began to gnaw on me. Living with a terminal illness was

6. Endoscopic retrograde cholangio pancreatography (ERCP) involved inserting a balloon or a stent into my main bile duct when my liver function tests were elevated, or when I was getting infections. Primary sclerosing cholangitis twists and scars the bile ducts, and the ERCP helps open them up and allows the bile to flow so the buildup of poisons can be expelled or neutralized through the liver.

no excuse to discount the fact that people were simply concerned about me. Having PSC was not a reason to put my own personal growth on hold. If anything, it was a great motivator to work on my shortcomings.

Even children saw my attitude as negative—including my own nieces, Alivia and Sonia. (My sister Kristy and my long-time friend Jeff Agli had met in 1999, married in 2000, and had Alivia in 2000 and Sonia in 2001.) My illness was illuminating traits that, before I was diagnosed, might have been looked at as gruff or impatient. But Alivia and Sonia put a different spin on it. Whenever they witnessed my curt exchanges with someone, they would respond, "Uncle Bubbie is cranky!" And I was! They were simply calling it like they saw it, because half the time when they saw me, I had a grimace on my face. Sure, I had reason to be crabby and, yes, children say the cutest things, but the fact that my little nieces were calling me "Cranky" was a warning signal. If I was going around snapping at people who cared about me, and if little children were commenting, then I had to admit it: My attitude stank.

The challenge for me was to improve my attitude, my approach, my mindset, about the effects of the disease I was living with. One way I felt I could start responding better was to work on my listening skills and respond to what was being said to me with less of a knee-jerk reaction. For instance, one day Jeff called me and asked if I would come over and help him move a television set. In my mind, I heard, *Hey, Bryan, can you help me move the TV? I hurt my back.* So I immediately rushed over and went downstairs to his basement, where they had a huge TV (the old kind that felt like they weighed a hundred pounds). I squatted down, grappled the thing up on my thighs and was wrestling to get my leg muscles to respond so I could straighten up.

"Whoa—whoa, there, Bryan," Jeff said and rushed to me. "Let me help you with that."

"No no," I barked, not wanting him to make his back any worse. "Back away—I've got it."

So I got the beast on my thighs and began lugging it up the stairs one groaning step at a time, like those crazy Scotsmen who toss telephone poles around.[7] Only I wasn't that strong. When I got almost to the top stair, I suddenly tripped and put a hole in the wall.

"Bryan, let me help you!" Jeff called out.

"Get away," I grunted. "I got this—*I got this*." I lowered the thing down—seeing stars, of course—and plopped down in a chair. "Oh my God," I groaned, "that thing weighs a ton."

"Bry," Jeff asked calmly, "why didn't you let me help you?"

"Because you told me you hurt your back," I said, my breath heaving.

"*What?* No no—I said I *didn't want to* hurt my back. That's why I asked you to come over and help me."

"Oh. I thought you said, '*Can you come over and help me move the TV because I hurt my back*' I thought that's what you said."

"No. No."

"Then why didn't you insist on helping me?"

"I *was* insisting," he said. "But you weren't listening."

Every muscle in my body was strained and on fire, and my brother-in-law and longtime friend was shaking his head in wonder at me, all because my communication skills needed improvement.

---

7. That was one of the imponderable mysteries of PSC: I could feel so ill one week and almost as healthy as a bull the next (although the healthy periods generally followed on the heels of my medical treatments).

There were too many other examples of my stubbornness, my curtness and my impatience for me to ignore. Like back in mid-1998 when I had first been diagnosed with PSC, I made the decision not to burden my younger sister, Amy, with the seriousness of my illness. By the time she came home that Christmas break, however, there was no more hiding it. The span of time from when she had left for college until the end of the year had revealed the ravage of the disease on me. Those who'd been around every day didn't notice my change as much, but for Amy it was dramatic. She cried. During her absence, I had become almost cadaver thin, and my eyes were yellow and hollow. It was traumatic for her.

In January, at the end of her Christmas break, I was in bed, dealing with the usual nausea and feeling emotionally down and defeated, when Amy timidly entered my room. "Bryan," she asked, "can I introduce my new friend Adam to you?"

"No!" I shot back.

My illness could turn me into a real crank sometimes. The positive mindset I had to adopt in order to survive, while medical specialists tried to keep me alive long enough to find a cure or a live donor, was often followed by periods of physical and emotional crashes that completely dampened my spirit. It was like living on a Ferris wheel. Up and down. Up and down. Amy had chosen one of those down days when I just wanted to be alone to rest and regroup. I didn't want to see anyone, let alone Amy's new boyfriend. I was in pain, I was nauseous, I was run down. How was I supposed to play the tough-guy skeptical older brother role when meeting her new boyfriend for the first time? So I snapped at her.

But as Amy turned to tiptoe out to tell her boyfriend I was in no shape to meet anyone, there came this tall, skinny shadow padding through my doorway.

"Nice ta meet ya," Adam announced in a Boston accent that couldn't help but put me in a better frame of mind.

"How ya doin'?" I responded.

"You doin' okay there?" he asked with genuine concern.

"Every day you wake up and are breathing God's good air," I replied, managing a grin, "you're doin' okay."

I liked the guy. Somehow I sensed Adam Martin was an ally.

So why had I gruffly barked at Amy when she'd only come to see me in simple joy over a new friend and wanted to share him with me? I had a lot of work to do on me.

Thankfully, I had great role models around me. My sister Kristy's boyfriend, Jeff, for example. Jeff had grown up in a dysfunctional family and was constantly amazed (as the "outsider looking in" on our family) that the Donahues all got along so well. We had our little disputes now and then, as all families do, but that was all they were, little disputes. We never left things festering. We would talk the issue through, blow off steam, and get back on track. Pressure never built up to blowout proportions. Our unspoken credo was, *Don't let the sun go down while you are still angry*.[8] Our close connection as a family was something Jeff never experienced when he was growing up. My parents, sisters and I were on the phone with one another on a daily basis, and we all got together for family dinners every Sunday and crashed at my parents' house afterward. Jeff loved it. When he married my sister Kristy, Jeff became family.

Jeff and I had history. We had known each other since we were kids. He was a few years older than me and lived across the

---

8. Ephesians 4:26; *New International Version* Bible.

street from my friend's house. Even before Jeff started dating Kristy, I looked up to him. He carried himself in a special way, did thoughtful things for others, set solid goals for himself. Jeff was the definition of "unique." His quiet, reserved thoughtfulness was anchored in a deep emotional reservoir of life experiences. He would set out to accomplish something and he would *do it*. Over the years, Jeff had become like a brother to me. He was well-rounded, dependable, an example to everyone. My admiration, love and respect for him had grown to the point where, if he and my sister Kristy ever squabbled, there was no way I could take a side.

As I began to ponder the fragility of my own life, and the importance of love and harmony and family, I realized that I wanted to be more like Jeff in many ways.

* * *

Dying will either make you grow, or make you bitter. No way was I going to allow it to make me bitter. There was much in me that needed attention—and not just physically. I didn't want to be any kind of a burden on anyone, for any reason. I wanted to be *normal*. And normal begins in the mind: the outlook, the mindset, the attitude, which (again) goes back to *choice*. Choice includes those little daily decisions we each must make to self-regulate our responses in order to overcome the natural human tendency to give in to the negative pressures that life continually throws our way. Sure, there were people in the world who had the ability to automatically make the most peaceful, positive, productive choices in their daily lives, people like the Dalai Lama, Mother Theresa, and even my own mom. But I was no Dalai Lama. Nor was I trying to be. I was just impatient to get over my impatience and be a little more gracious with the concerns of others about my health, while not being the focus of constant hand-wringing worry. After all, their intentions were only to do something to make my plight easier. But to my thinking, the thing that would have made it easier would have been to just quit bugging me—and that's where I needed improvement. It was time to upgrade my communication skills, nip the sarcasm, bite my tongue, and respond better to the motives of those around me. They weren't bugging me, they were *loving* me. I was determined to love them back with grace, compassion, and appreciation for their good intentions.

It was becoming increasingly important to me that people would remember me in a positive light as they gathered around my casket. It was about *legacy*. It was about giving back. I didn't want to be thought of as negative or crabby or cranky. Those were habits and attitudes that I wanted to break. Inside, I had the best of intentions. It was time to focus on bringing those intentions to the forefront, to make them a natural part of my everyday words, actions and reactions. After all, every day I was above ground was a good day.

My mom always reinforced that idea that nobody is entitled to anything. "There is no entitlement out there in this world," she would tell us. "You have to work for it, earn it, or get it by the grace of God." That credo also applies to our health. For example, we are not automatically entitled to be fit and in shape. If we want that, we can't go around eating everything we want whenever we want and never exercise. I began to realize that the same credo also applied to my situation. I wasn't entitled to be instantly free of PSC. I *wanted* to be free of it, of course, but there was no automatic entitlement to it. I could either sit on my duff and hope that, by the grace of God, I would be free of PSC, or I could vigorously join in the battle and do whatever I could to beat my PSC and regain my health. I couldn't medically do much beyond what Dr. Kaplan and his team were already doing to prolong my life while they searched for a cure. And I couldn't count on miraculously working my way quickly to the top of the years-long liver donor list. However, I could try to learn about non-surgical ways to augment the medical efforts underway on my behalf. As it turned out, I was already on the right track, because what I could do mostly pertained to deliberately choosing a positive mental attitude.

Stress, Health and Happiness[9]

Stress plays a major role in our physical health. When we are under stress, the body reacts as if it were under actual physical assault—which triggers internal system defense mechanisms.[10] If activated too frequently, these mechanisms can cause long-term health problems, including increased susceptibility to infection, ulcers, cardiovascular disease and possibly even cancer. Studies show that stress is increasing at an alarming rate in young men, with one in four young men in America at serious risk of developing stress related illnesses.[11]

One of the conclusions drawn by the authors of the *Handbook of Health Psychology* is that major stressful experiences are associated with changes in immune function.[12] The most recent

---

9. The source for much of this material comes from: http://www. knowledgeworkerperformance.com/Articles/Stress-Happiness-Body.aspx
10. Michael Argyle (2001), *The Psychology of Happiness* (Taylor & Francis, Second Ed.).
11. S. McNamara (2000), "Stress in Young People: What's New and What Can We Do?" (London: Continuum); and S. McNamara (2001), "Stress Management Program for Secondary School Students" (London: Routledge Falmer).
12. Andrew Baum, Tracey A. Revenson, Jerome E. Singer, *Handbook of Health Psychology* (Lawrence Erlbaum Associates, Publishers, 2001), 691.

research indicates that primary sclerosing cholangitis is related to the auto-immune system (though that hasn't been confirmed). There is also evidence of a link between stress and the suppression of the body's natural killer-cells (one function of which is to protect the body against the development of malignant tumors).[13] In fact, studies have found that stress is related to *many* diseases and illnesses, and brings with it an increased risk of cardiovascular and coronary artery disease.[14] What was most encouraging to me was that the medical community is increasingly accepting the influence of the mind on health, through fields such as psychoneuroimmunology. A 1987 study revealed that:

> "Stressors . . . weaken the immune system on the day they occur. Pleasant events enhanced the immune system for up to two days. A drop in pleasant events predicted increased susceptibility to the common cold more accurately than an increase in unpleasant events. This makes sense if one sees the body as a holistic system where thoughts release chemicals into the body, in turn affecting metabolism and *immune system function*. There are two aspects to this. The first is the workings of the nervous system, in particular the brain, which determines how we feel about things that happen to us. The second is the way the body defends itself when the brain determines that a major issue is in play. This is the stress response, and is triggered by intense events, both distressing and pleasant.

---

13. A 1984 study conducted by Noun Shavit and Claude Afalo; see: http://en.wikipedia.org/wiki/Health
14. T.G. Dinan (2001), "Stress, Depression and Cardiovascular Disease"; *Stress & Health: Journal of the International Society of Investigating Stress 17(2)*, 65-66.

*Less intense emotions allow the body to continue
to work optimally"* (italics added).[15]

If stress alone was an indicator of potential serious physical
health problems, then I was past the ticking time bomb stage. But
the hopeful news was that reducing the intensity of my somewhat
negative emotional responses could actually help my body in its
efforts to function normally. It wouldn't cure the PSC in me, but
it was confirmation that more positive responses to stimuli could
actually help. There were also studies that showed that different
stimuli in the brain trigger neurotransmitter chemicals that affect
the brain state to actually induce positive emotions:[16]

> **Serotonin**: Induces alertness, positive mood and sociabil-
> ity, and acts against depression.
> **Dopamine**: Believed to activate the links between the
> amygdala (which determines emotional response) and
> the frontal cortex (which expresses emotional response).
> Dopamine is important in rewarding the brain for acting
> on certain stimuli, such as eating, sex, etc.
> **Endorphins**: Provide feelings of euphoria and reduce
> pain. These are produced by exercise, among other
> things.
> **GABA**: An inhibitor that reduces anxiety.

In short, happiness can actually allow the body to recover
from stress. So I began to choose deliberate happiness. I chose

---

15. Summary of A.A. Stone, B.R. Reed and J.M. Neale (1987); *Journal of Human
    Stress* (p. 70–74), as found at "Stress, Happiness and Their Impact on Our
    Bodies" (http://www.knowledgeworkerperformance.com/Articles/Stress-
    Happiness-Body.aspx)
16. See: http://www.knowledgeworkerperformance.com/Articles/Stress-Happiness-
    Body.aspx

to look at the glass as *full*. Not half full, not half empty, but *full to the brim*.

Further studies showed that an intense emotional response or stressor of any kind results in the activation of the "sympathetic nervous system," which includes an initial alarm response that brings the body's defensive forces to bear on a problem. If the stressor were to persist, then the body would adapt to the continuing stress. There was further hope offered in the conclusion of the *Handbook of Health Psychology*:

"Individuals differ substantially in the magnitude of their immunologic responsivity to stress, with recent evidence suggesting that these response tendencies may reflect attributes of individuals."[17]

My "attributes" included a stubborn hardheadedness and a refusal to accept anything I categorically disagreed with. Such as the perception that I was going to die of PSC. Not on my watch, I wasn't.

Now I had even more reason to follow my instincts about the role our mind plays in lowering stress and improving our health. It all went back to choice. And I chose *life*.

The Rule of Regret

Life is not a dress rehearsal—we get *one* shot at it. I realized that, even with my dwindling shot, I had to get out there as much as I could and live my life to the fullest.

Lia and I decided early on that we would never again experience a time when we were on the fence about something we wanted to do but weren't sure if we should or could do it—only

---

17. Andrew Baum, Tracey A. Revenson, Jerome E. Singer, *Handbook of Health Psychology* (Lawrence Erlbaum Associates, Publishers, 2001), 691.

to realize that when we decided not to do it, we regretted it. We developed a rule that we lived by on the weekends. We called it The Rule of Regret. If we felt we might regret on Monday morning something we could have done on the weekend but didn't, then we would force ourselves to do it right then and there.

One Saturday afternoon, Lia and I were canoeing on a beautiful, hot, summer day.

"I'd love to jump in," I said casually as I dipped my oar in and out of the water.

"Then go for it," she responded.

As I was thinking about whether I really wanted to be wet for the rest of the day, she suddenly invoked the Rule of Regret on me: "You're going to regret it if you don't do it," she smiled.

Before I knew it, we were both in the water. It was the highlight of our day.

The Zone

When we become bigger than our problems, we control them. But when we let our problems become bigger than us, we will lose. Life is all about the power of thought in controlling the choices we make every day to succeed. One of the choices I made was to *stop worrying*. A simple rule of thumb I had always tried to live by was that I would not allow myself to worry about two days in the week: *yesterday* and *tomorrow*. I would have died from stress long before my liver got the best of me if I hadn't started living by that mindset. I forced myself not to stress out or worry about those two days. I lived for today only, and made that day the best day I possibly could. I knew I could not change yesterday; but if I won today, then tomorrow would take care of itself.

I was learning to choose to live in "The Zone," that place beyond our standard comfort zones. (It's amazing the vibrant hues and tones the world takes on when viewed through the lens of time quickly ticking away.) We've all heard the saying, Stop and smell the roses. Once I got in The Zone, I actually began to do just that. Each day I hadn't succumbed to PSC was another day I was robbing death, so I literally *stopped and smelled roses* when I came across them. I started stopping to enjoy the simple things that most of us tend to take for granted or overlook in our hectic everyday lives. I developed rituals that kept me focused on the task at hand, on who or what was in front of me, on what I was doing in the moment. I found that the key to the rituals was to know when they were working and when they needed to be adjusted. And I applied the rituals in focusing on staying alive long enough to find a live donor or a cure to PSC. "Nothing is impossible" became my mantra—even though, by Christmas of 2002, live donor transplants were still relatively new for PSC patients. Nevertheless, Dr. Kaplan and his team had been keeping me alive with their experimental program for more than four years.

Still, I was only human. I had my bad days, too. Fortunately for me, I had a strong support group around me that would rally behind me and carry me through the rough patches. There were times when I was so sick that I woke up feeling miserable, and a bad attitude would grip me. I would stay in bed, unable to keep food down, the physical pain crushing me, limiting me, sometimes stopping me like a board in the face. During days like those, my illness was much worse because I wasn't controlling it; I was letting it control me. I knew that if I allowed PSC to win, then my day was finished—negativity would fill the void and take over. Then the constant mantra tattooed to my mind would kick in: *Don't let it break you! If you break, you lose!* And I would drag myself up from bed and haul myself out into the world, physical pain, mental struggle and all.

Battling daily to keep death at bay, while trying to appear as normal as possible to the outside world, was exhausting. I thought a lot about my life, my attitudes and approaches to people, and my constant desire to figure out how to leave a positive legacy. It was entirely up to me to make the decision every day if it was going to be a good day or a bad one. Because only my mind could really keep negativity at bay. Yet, negative was normal in my state, as my body was unable to naturally filter out toxins and poisons. Whether I was excited to go to bed at night and equally excited to get up in the morning was my sole choice, no matter how positive and encouraging people around me were. From the instant I awoke each morning, I would mentally psych myself up to engage in the fight to win. It was war! Whatever I decided in the first ten minutes when my eyes opened each morning would determine my fate for that entire day. Physically, I may have been at the mercy of the illness; but emotionally and mentally, *I* was in charge—I controlled whether I would win.

* * *

As 2002 drew to a close, I had been in and out of the hospital several times, but continued to work hard at keeping up my public facade of health. I never talked about my sickness. Other than my immediate family, no one knew I was living with a terminal illness. I didn't stop my lifestyle. I even continued going out with my friends.[18]

---

18. I drank cranberry juice when I went out. I'd stopped drinking alcohol back when I was diagnosed in 1998.

By late 2002, Lia was working on her master's in psychology and was employed as a research assistant, doing neuroscience research for Yale University. After college, I had gotten a job as an insurance claims adjustor, but I was antsy to get a more challenging job.

That December, I had a job interview for the position of mortgage loan officer with a North Haven company called United Mortgage. Kelly McGuinness, the president and owner, was a smart woman with a friendly, no-nonsense demeanor and a heart of pure platinum. I met some of the staff, including her husband Jay, the company's chief financial officer. I had a great feeling about the company and the people working there. And I had absolutely no experience for the position.

Kelly told me to report for work the first week of January. It was a challenge I was hungry for. I not only wanted the work, but I also needed the stimulation and the opportunity to ignore my disease.

After going through an intensive two week training session, I told Kelly, "I think you should fire me."

"Why's that?" Kelly chuckled.

"Because I am never going to remember all this stuff."

It wasn't long before I began to feel like I had won the employment lotto. The employees were amazing. Kelly and Jay were an incredible couple.

Still, I made the decision not to let anyone at United Mortgage know that I had PSC. I chose not to disclose my physical situation to them because I didn't want to be treated differently than the others. I was gradually losing weight, but I hoped that since they were seeing me every day, they wouldn't notice the decline, and that jaundice wouldn't be familiar to them. I was naive enough to think nobody outside of my family would notice

I was so sick. They'd never met me before, so they didn't know if I was just another skinny guy. I was hoping they were thinking things like, *He must be a vegan. Long distance runner. Not much of an appetite.*

I took extreme measures to hide my situation from everybody at the office. For example, lunchtime at the office was a big deal. The calls started over the intercom at 10:30 in the morning as to which restaurant we were ordering from. The menu always sounded great, too. But I knew that if I ate, I would soon be puking sick in front of my coworkers (I was usually exhausted by noon anyway). So I used the excuse that I had to go home to walk my dog, Lucy. While my coworkers sat around and ate and yakked and bonded and laughed and discussed world events and joked with one another, I was at home, eating something light and then taking a nap so I would have the energy to finish my workday.

Yet, in spite of my good attitude and ongoing efforts to stay positive and healthy, I was down to 130 pounds—I'd dropped a total of seventy pounds. I was having fluid drained from my stomach every week and stents and balloons inserted in my common bile duct on a regular basis. I would schedule my doctor visits or hospital procedures on Fridays so I could tell my coworkers I was taking a long weekend. I'd have the procedure on Friday and recover during the weekend so I could be back at work on Monday (pretending as if I had enjoyed a fun-filled weekend).

What I didn't know at the time, however, was that Kelly and Jay McGuinness already knew plenty about liver disease.

* * *

On almost a daily basis with the liver disease, I experienced fatigue, jaundice, dull to intense pain, itchiness, and loss of weight and appetite. The fatigue was not just tiredness, it was waking up in the morning feeling like I had just run a marathon—I was drop-dead exhausted. Sometimes it took an hour just to coax and pump myself up out of bed. I would need to rest or take constant little naps during the day—and I'd still have little or no energy afterward. Everything I ate made me sick. And although I'd lost a lot of weight, I did whatever I could not to look malnourished—even though my eyes were yellow from the jaundice and my skin looked like it was glowing. The pain I felt was not mere discomfort, it was a stabbing pain. I would sweat through my clothes. The itching felt like it was *inside* of my body. I would scratch until I bled, trying to get it out. And all of this was a result of the bile that was supposed to flow through my liver, but was instead backing up in my system and gushing into my bloodstream.

That was my life. Day in, day out. Little did I know it then, but that was as good as it was going to get, too. I was advised to go on disability (and I certainly qualified for it), but I wasn't *disabled*; I was just battling to regain my life and health. Most of all, I was determined to win this war—without whining along the way.

Throughout 2003 and 2004, I continued to go to Boston every three or four months for my regular treatments, and whenever I was suddenly in extreme pain and sickness—and that frequency was increasing dramatically.

During one ERCP procedure, my mother and father tiptoed into my room at the hospital and watched as I lay there under anesthesia. To them, I looked dead. The surgeons had put my diagnostic images up and explained to them: I was reaching a critical point in the progression of the disease. PSC was simply beating me down. It was constantly one step forward and two back. Yet, I refused to give up. Although it had been a long and painful process that was constantly "touch and go," through Dr. Kaplan's treatments and the ongoing hospital visits and insertions of stents, physicians had managed to keep me alive well past the initial estimate of "six months to live." If the average lifespan of a person diagnosed with PSC was nine or ten years, then I still had a good three or four years left in me.

I had a life to build.

An American Family

Family, love and life are all the more precious when time grows short. I wanted every remaining minute with each of my family members to be nothing but uplifting and as normal as possible.

Lia and I became like second parents to Jeff and Kristy's little girls, Alivia and Sonia. To them, I was "Bubbie." They would call me and say, "Bubbie, we need Dairy Queen!" And I would run to the Dairy Queen and get them some ice cream and take it to them. Then it became, "Bubbie, Mommy wants Dairy Queen, too!" And I'd go and fetch ice cream for my sister. I didn't know any other way. Because love is not only a verb, it's also a choice—and so is expressing and communicating words and actions of love.

As my illness advanced and the treatments increased and became more difficult for the doctors to do, I began to see people from a different vantage point. I looked inside each of my relationships and began working to improve the ones that needed work. I turned those relationships upside down, looked only at their positive attributes and built on those, while deliberately suppressing old judgmental tendencies within me. Soon, people who used to drive me crazy, I was now finding enjoyable to be around.

I was also abundantly blessed by countless relationships that needed no work whatsoever, with people who were simply amazing. In 1999, when Amy's boyfriend, Adam, graduated from college (a year ahead of Amy), he moved back home to Lowell, Massachusetts, and they carried on a long-distance relationship. Adam so loved Amy that he would never have asked her to move away from her family to be closer to him; he wanted her to remain near me, her sister, nieces and parents. That was Adam, an incredible young man who recognized that the whole family was the Donahue focal point—my disease never was the center of our attention. Adam never saw much of what I was dealing with. He only saw the Donahue family, of which I was but a part, having fun and enjoying my life. Adam never fully realized how sick I was. What he saw and came to love was a solid American family.

I refused to let the illness stop me from living life. In 2004, Amy and Adam got married and bought a new house. The day they closed on the loan, Adam and I gutted the kitchen together. I was all hammers and elbows, tearing down walls. Nobody could stop me. I chose to be there, to help out, to get my hands dirty. It was a work ethic I'd inherited from my father, sure, but it was also a great way to keep my focus off of the disease ravaging my liver, and instead focus on *living*. When you can combine vigorous living with helping those you love, that's practically heaven on Earth.

The Small Stuff

As 2003 headed to a close, I was at the ripe old age of twenty-seven and was finally learning to never sweat the small stuff. It's easy to lose track of our true priorities in life and start worrying about the small things, because everything is relative to what we are going through at any particular moment. But we get into our routines and we start forgetting priorities and we begin to sweat the small stuff. When that happens, we have to bring ourselves back and remind ourselves that this trial is actually not such a big deal. There are worse things that can happen in life—especially knowing that it can be over so suddenly.

As I began to sense that my time was probably growing short, I started to think about those I loved, and I wondered if they would be okay after I passed away. Amy had grown into a remarkable young lady. After graduating, she became a school teacher, teaching children with learning disabilities. She was a wonderful wife to Adam, and would be a mother equal to Kristy some day—one equal to our own mother. I could only hope that their tears at my death would not be tears of sadness, but of happiness at how much I admired and loved Amy and Kristy both. In the Donahue family, we tended not to say the words *I love you* to each other too often, because our love for one another was something we simply knew was the constant undercurrent, the overtone, the backdrop to our lives together. We *felt* it; we *knew* it. We lived it.

When you have a mystifying, incurable disease like PSC, you learn to thank God for the blessing of family like Kristy and Jeff, and Amy and Adam, and my mom and dad. I could never even begin to express the depth and richness of my love for my mother and father. I was determined to keep fighting to the very end so I could enjoy their presence for every precious remaining moment. I was determined to use the rest of my time to pass forward the foundation of love and family togetherness that my parents had made such a solid part of my upbringing.

* * *

Amy came to see me during one of my trips to the hospital in Boston while she was still in college. It was extremely difficult for her, because there I was, her big brother, protector and hero, dying. I was supposed to be there for her, to take care of her, my little sister. I forced back the realization that one day soon I would have to sit down and write her a letter. How do you tell your beloved little sister that you have to leave her—*permanently*—but that things will be okay? How do you write a goodbye letter to the mother who bore you? The father who taught you so much about strength, leadership and the true meaning of being a man? How do you tell your older sister she was always more like a wonderful friend to you than a sister? All I could think of was how grateful I was that my sisters had husbands like Jeff and Adam to love them and care for them.

After her visit with me in Boston, Amy returned to school numbed and in shock at my rapid deterioration. This was just one of an increasing number of close calls.

One of those close calls came a few months later, when I was again admitted to Tufts in Boston, scheduled for yet another ERCP procedure. Lia and my mother took me and, as usual, booked a hotel room across the street from the hospital. I went in for the operation while they waited in the waiting room. It was standard procedure for me. The surgical team would go in, insert a stent that would open up the bile duct and allow the bile to flow properly for awhile. Usually, I would go in on a Friday, have the surgery done, and a week or so later, go back and have the stent removed.[19] I'd gone through the procedure many times before.

But this time, things were different. When I got out of recovery I was nearly comatose from the anesthesia, so instead of making

---

19. Unlike a heart stent, which can be left in the patient, a bile stent must be removed and replaced.

the long drive back home, we decided to spend the night at a hotel. I went to bed and slept like a baby from the meds. But Lia and my mom didn't sleep a wink. Because they knew what I did not: I hadn't had a stent or balloon inserted. Those days were over.

While I was in post-op, a resident had approached my mom and wife. "We were unable to insert a stent or a balloon this time," he stated bluntly. "Because the block is not in the main bile duct." He explained that the ducts inside my liver had become so twisted and scarred that it was now impossible to even reach them to try and open them up.

"What do we do?" Lia asked him. "What are the next steps?"

"What should we do to help relieve his pain and discomfort?" my mom added.

The resident seemed surprised by the questions. His answer was delivered with an undertone that said, *How can you not understand what I'm telling you?* What he was trying to tell them was that there was nothing else they could do for me. This was it. This was the nature of my illness and where it was always headed. In a clinical and dispassionate way, the resident essentially indicated that they needed to wake up, there was nothing more they could do. *There is no help here. Bryan is done.*

Although everyone knew I was sick, they never thought it would actually get to the point where I would either have a transplant or I would die. It was now at that point. My mom and Lia were shocked, numb, confused. They insisted on seeing Dr. Kaplan immediately, refusing to leave until they spoke with him in person.

Dr. Kaplan arrived and had a talk with the doctor and the resident. Then he said, in an uncharacteristically solemn tone, "It's time to *seriously* look for a liver donor."

The stopgap measures were no longer working. My days above ground were drawing to a close.

CHAPTER 7

The Wolf at the Door

As 2004 began and the PSC continued its relentless advance, I was forced to face the reality that another major shift in my health was on the horizon—hopefully, a miraculous movement up the liver donor wait list (although jumps like that were generally proceeded by a knock on heaven's door). While I was at least able to get myself back and forth to work two times a day, the increasing interruptions caused by my hospital visits were becoming difficult to hide or explain away. My coworkers who saw me each day at the office couldn't have known that I wasn't eating well and that I was napping during my lunch breaks, because they were used to seeing me all the time, which made them less aware of my gradual weight loss or how withdrawn I was. They'd seen the jaundice all along, but to them, that was just Bryan. Even Lia eventually became accustomed to the decline.

But I could no longer hold off telling my boss, Kelly McGuinness, owner of United Mortgage. By the summer of 2004, Kelly and I had developed a great friendship. She was stunned as I explained the extent of my health situation to her.

"Why didn't you tell me before?" she asked.

Her tone of voice was far more one of alarm and concern for me than of displeasure that I'd withheld a pretty important piece of information about myself during my interview. But, *Can I have a job—Oh, by the way, I have a terminal illness*, isn't something you want to bring up at a job interview, especially if you were refusing to acknowledge the disease like I was. Kelly revealed to me why she was so alarmed that I hadn't said a word to her or her husband, Jay, about my liver disease: Jay's mother had died in

1999 just five weeks after being diagnosed with cancer of the liver. Prior to that, when Jay was a child, his mother had primary biliary cirrhosis (a hardening of the liver's bile ducts—not dissimilar from my bile duct disease). Doctors discussed the possibility of doing a liver transplant, but in those days, it was a complex operation and was rarely performed. Then, incredibly, her condition went dormant and she was told she might have months or even years to live. She lived into her seventies. Then the biliary cirrhosis mysteriously reappeared and was cancerous. By the time she became symptomatic, it was too late to even think about a transplant.

However, PSC was different. It was far more deadly, never went into remission, and it could turn into cancer as well. My news instantly moved me into a whole new dimension of relationship with Kelly and Jay McGuinness.

In his office at United Mortgage, Jay had a photo of a golf foursome that had been taken nearly a year earlier. One of the four was me. As I finished telling Kelly and Jay about my health problem, Jay looked from me to the photo and back. In the picture, I was thin and had sunken eyes. "That's the everyday Bryan I know," he murmured, dumbstruck at the fact that I looked even worse less than one year later. "You look totally different now than you did then. How could I not have seen you were sick?"

They just never knew what the healthy Bryan looked like.

* * *

By 2005, with the accelerating decline in my health, I needed to relieve some of the increasing personal stress that the illness was creating. The manager above me who reported to Kelly had recently left the company, and Kelly and Jay had taken the opportunity to begin reorganizing the firm. The commercial and residential mortgage industry was booming at the time, so the manager's departure offered me perfect timing to approach Kelly with an unusual request.

"What would you think about putting me on salary?" I asked her. Kelly knew what I was living with. She knew my symptoms were deteriorating rapidly, doctors had run out of options, and the treatments at Tufts were no longer effective. "Working on commission is—"

"—I know," she nodded, reading my thoughts. "A fluctuating income is tough for your peace of mind when you're distracted by bigger issues."

Even in a good economy, it wasn't easy to gauge how much money you were going to make from one month to the next. My request was a long shot because the company had never before put anyone on salary. But I needed to bring some stability to Lia and my finances, and take some worry off of my mind. And there was no way I was going to just retire on disability, have a goodbye pizza party at the office, and go sit at home on death watch during my final few months.

After talking it over with Jay, Kelly announced her decision. In the reorganization of United Mortgage, she factored in my experience, education and qualifications, and made me a manager. This took a huge stress off of my mind—and it opened the door for Kelly and me to make the transition from being friendly at work to becoming friends.

Working for Kelly McGuinness was incredible. I could not have been hired to work for a better person, a better company, a better family. I had hidden my illness from her (and everyone at United Mortgage) because I didn't want to be treated any differently than anyone else in the company. Yet, true to form, Kelly did exactly that, going above and beyond for me, and making my days much easier to endure. But that was Kelly—she always did far more for all of her employees than she'd ever give herself credit for. As a small business owner, there were many things she could not do that large corporations could, but one of the benefits of running a small business was that you could more readily meet people's needs on a personal level.[20] Kelly believed that life and family were more important than business and work, but that when they were approached with a healthy balance, the result was a richer world all around. After all, one happy employee was more productive than a dozen disgruntled ones.

Kelly also felt that America had become such a litigious environment that it made it difficult to do something special for one employee without having to do the same for everyone. Just the thought of the cost of litigation for smaller firms was enough to cause them to back down and not offer help to employees with unusual needs. But Kelly was different. Even if it meant that the financial resources to help me were to come directly out of her own pocket, with no performance quid pro quo on my part, she would have done it anyway. She believed that's what we're supposed to do for each other in this world; rise up and just do it. Kelly even made sure that I had health care insurance that would allow my doctors and medical specialists to be included in the plan at no additional cost to me. Bosses simply don't do those sorts of things in this day and age of misplaced corporate priorities. Kelly's above-and-beyond generosity made me deeply loyal to her, to her family, and to the company.

Kelly and Jay McGuinness were having an incredible influence on my outlook. Their attitude and the way they treated

---

20. As just one small example, Kelly had single mothers working for her who needed to be able to take phone calls throughout the day from their children. Kelly allowed that. In a large corporation, taking personal time during work hours would be frowned upon, if not outright prohibited.

me, added significantly to shaping and building me. Kelly's ways of caring for others without stopping to measure the cost of the effort or the worth of the recipient is what America should be all about.

* * *

By the summer of 2005, my hospital visits had increased to every other week, sometimes more. Everything was getting worse—my appetite, my weight, my physical pain and discomfort. My liver function tests were elevated. I often became feverish at odd hours. To try to keep me nourished, Lia made every kind of food I had once enjoyed, but I could only stomach things like Cup O'Noodles soup. I couldn't imagine what she was going through as she watched her husband slowly dying, even as I fought every day to function as if I were normal.

That July, I was moved up the organ transplant list. Doctors advised me to get my affairs in order and to find a live donor *soon*, because by the time I gained enough seniority on the regular liver donor list, it would be too late.[21] At that point, I knew it was just about over. I would continue the fight as long as I could. Then I would die. Because I simply would not ask someone perfectly healthy to give me a piece of an organ they needed to live—and put their life and health in jeopardy in the process.

One of my biggest problems (*assets* might be a better word) had always been my stubbornness. In fact, I don't think I ever failed to accomplish anything I had set out to complete. Except my life. My life had some interesting twists and turns. Before I got sick,

---

21. Rather than a fresh cadaver liver, by this time, live liver donor operations were being done on PSC patients. A part of a living liver could be transplanted from donor to recipient (a highly risky operation for both); over time, a full liver would re-grow in each person.

I was headed in one direction. When I got sick, it was abruptly shoved into another. What I never revealed after I was diverted in this new direction was that my motivation for trying to live life with a positive mindset was plain old *fear*. I wasn't John Wayne or Gandhi. I was just a regular guy, trying to deal with a terrifying real-life issue. I was afraid of not having a chance to live, afraid that my life would be gone before I'd had an opportunity to have a positive impact on anyone, or to leave behind some good piece of "me" for the world.

After I was diagnosed with PSC, my regret was that I hadn't really been living for those first twenty-two years of my life. I longed to be able to step back, look at my life and say, "Hey, I accomplished that." Instead, my philosophical discussion became, *Maybe I shouldn't expect to have accomplished much at this young age anyway.* But that only introduced the question, "At what age should a person begin making efforts to achieve something significant, or to meet noteworthy milestones? And should age matter at all?" Maybe I actually had accomplished important things by then in my life, but I wasn't looking at them as significant. I started to have a hard time with the fact that I might die soon . . . and what did I contribute during my short life? When I looked at my life's contribution (if any), was it a *good* contribution? Even though I was still only in my twenties, there had to be some contribution back to the world, because I could not accept that our lives are to be lived in busy, endless, self-gratifying "doing," with little or no focus on how our activity benefits others. Otherwise, we're no different than animals foraging a lifetime for daily food, and then dying.

I was not an animal. I wasn't *crippled*. And I did not want to die.

It was at that point that I decided that I had to run with it and do everything I could to make a contribution. That required that I not cease my fight to really *live*. To live a life that would serve as a good example, while also being a life of joy and vibrancy. That's a huge goal when you've just been told there's nothing else the doctors can do for you. But when you're in your twenties and dying, you want to try to bring a positive message to anyone you come into contact with, because you only just arrived on Earth, and suddenly time is ebbing.

To accomplish all of that quickly, I couldn't have any negative anything around me—including people feeling pity for me, or seeing me as a killjoy. So how in the world could I be positive and hopeful while going around asking for a piece of somebody's liver? How do you ask someone to take a risk that is at least as dangerous to the donor as to the patient receiving the gift (because both donor and recipient are at risk of dying from the operation)? How do you explain that they'd be left with ill health for months (if they even survived the operation) and that they'd have a scar from their abdomen up their chest that would look like a hammerhead shark took a chunk out of them during a Sunday swim?

As the summer of 2005 came to a close, I had made no headway whatsoever in locating a live donor. I hadn't asked anybody—I couldn't. If I didn't get serious, doctors warned, I would be dead by Thanksgiving, Christmas at the latest. Period. Measure me for a coffin.

With a mixture of apologetic reluctance and purposeful anticipation, we asked family members and only the very closest of friends. A longtime friend named Todd, who had married my cousin Melissa, was a match, but his cholesterol was too high.

Doctors said they might consider him if they absolutely had to. So Todd went on a diet, hoping to get his cholesterol down. And we kept looking.

My parents were tested. My father wasn't a match. My sisters didn't match.

My mother was a match, but she was too small. She didn't understand when doctors kept saying, "Yes, you're a match, but your size might be a problem."

"My size?" she asked. "Do you want me to gain weight? Because that's what I'll do—whatever it takes."

The doctor explained that because she was much smaller than me, her liver would more than likely be too small. The liver grows to fill the space of the cavity in the body. A sufficient amount is necessary so the liver can get a good start growing in the recipient. But if too much liver has to be taken from the donor, it may not grow quickly enough to sustain both donor and recipient in the crucial weeks and months after the operation.

"I would give him my right arm without anesthesia," my mother insisted, on the verge of tears. "Tell me what to do."

"We might consider you only if it comes down to the wire and we're unable to find a donor at the last hour," the doctor responded.

"We've lived our whole lives," my dad said. "If my liver only matched . . ." his voice trailed off as he started to choke up. "You know you could have it."

* * *

By the time 2005 wound down, Dr. Kaplan had kept me alive for nearly eight years with his experimental medication and the insertion of bile duct stents and balloons at Tufts. In the first few years after I was initially diagnosed, I had responded well enough that I had been taken off of the liver transplant list. However, the drug treatments and the hospital procedures had only been slowing down the advance of the disease, but it was still in me. The tide had now reversed. Slowing the advance of the PSC was over. We'd run out of options. I would be at end-stage liver failure before the year was out.

Merry Christmas.

I put my affairs in order. The transplant team and my doctors called my family in for a final meeting.[22]

In September of 2005, Tufts New England Medical Center assigned a transplant coordinator to help us search for a live donor. In preparation for the hope that a donor might miraculously be found *real* soon, the coordinator set up meetings for us with a variety of people—psychiatrists, physical therapists, nutritionists, as was customary for transplant operations.

At the family meeting at the hospital, the coordinator explained what to expect from a live donor operation and the types of risks such a procedure would entail.

The Living Donor Liver Transplant[23]

As many as 500 patients have living donor transplants every year in America; more than 6,000 transplanted livers come from deceased donors. However, there are 18,000 people in America

---

22. Yet, I continued working—my attitude so bucked against reality that I had convinced myself that *I would win*.
23. The source for much of the information in this section comes from Dilip Moonka, Sammy Saab and James Trotter, "Living Donor Liver Transplantation" (American Society of Transplantation, May 7, 2007); see: www.a-s-t.org; and the "Primary Sclerosing Cholangitis" study by Marshall M. Kaplan, M.D. (February 6, 1998); and the April 6, 1995 *New England Journal of Medicine* article titled "Medical Progress: Primary Sclerosing Cholangitis." For a succinct description of the details of the actual operation, see: *To The Edge And Back* by Chris Klug (Carroll & Graf Publishers, 2004), chapter 16, "The Operation."

on the waiting list for a liver transplant, with more patients added every day. In fact, more than 1,700 patients die each year just while waiting.

Living donor transplants were first done in the 1980s in children as a way to shorten the long wait times for a liver.[24] Because the surgery can be planned in advance, the chances of a successful transplant are increased and the quality of the donated liver may be better because living donors are usually younger, healthier adults. However, with a living donor transplant, the preservation time (the length of time the liver can be without blood before needing to be transplanted) is usually only minutes, instead of hours (as with cadaver donors).

Liver transplants are given to patients on the basis of how sick they are. Each patient waiting for a liver transplant is given a score called the "Model for End-Stage Liver Disease" (MELD). Calculation of the MELD score is based on such factors as age, blood type, condition of the liver, and several other criteria; the resulting MELD score determines a patient's place on the cadaver liver transplant list. Patients with a higher MELD score are in more advanced stages of need, and thus have a higher chance of getting a liver transplant sooner.

With organ transplants, safety is paramount for both the donor and the recipient, and the risk of death as a result of the transplant and related complications is very real. Liver donors are required to go through a medical exam to ensure that their liver is healthy and that it's safe for them to donate.

---

24. Approximately half of all livers for pediatric liver transplants come from living donors. More adults are receiving living donor transplants as well, because many adult patients cannot survive the wait times for a deceased donor liver.

In general, liver donors must:

- Be at least eighteen years old.
- Have an emotional tie with the recipient.
- Have a compatible blood type to the recipient.
- Have a fairly similar body size as the recipient.
- Be a non-smoker for at least four to six weeks before surgery.
- Be in good health with no major medical or mental illnesses.
- Be able to understand and follow instructions before and after surgery.

The Donor Medical Evaluation

A person who wants to donate part of his or her liver must go through a complete medical evaluation (including blood work, radiology studies, and a liver biopsy) to make sure the potential donor does not have any health issues that could increase the risk of problems during and after surgery, and to make sure the size of the donated portion of liver is a compatible size and shape for the recipient.

The testing process for donors includes the following as part of the medical evaluation:

- **Blood tests:** The first test is to find out if the donor's blood type matches the recipient's blood type.
- **Physical exam:** If the donor's and recipient's blood types match, the donor will get a physical examination.
- **Virus and disease tests:** The donor is tested for viruses such as hepatitis B, hepatitis C, and HIV; for common liver diseases; and for diabetes or other diseases.

- **Functions:** The transplant team measures liver and kidney function, as well as red and white blood cell and blood platelet counts.
- **Ultrasound/MRI/CAT scan:** These tests are done to get images of the liver to make sure the donor's bile ducts, arteries and veins are the right fit for the intended recipient. These pictures will also look for benign and malignant tumors (which are sometimes discovered during this process).
- **Chest X-ray and EKG:** These are standard tests done before any major operation, to check for lung or heart problems.
- **Consultations:** Every donor will meet with a social worker or psychiatrist to talk about their reasons for donating a liver and to make sure they are in a stable mental condition for the surgery, and are not being pressured in any way to donate their liver. (It is against the law for people to sell their body parts; no money may be exchanged for the donation of a liver.)

It usually takes between two and four weeks for a donor to go through these tests. In an emergency, however, the tests can be done in as little as forty-eight hours. Once this evaluation process is begun, the donor can back out at any time for any reason.

The Transplant Surgery

The donor's liver is split into two parts. One part is removed for the transplant. Both livers begin to heal and grow new tissue, growing back to normal size within six to eight weeks.

The Hospital Stay

Donors stay in the hospital anywhere from four to seven days after surgery (longer if problems occur). The first night after surgery is spent in the intensive care unit.

Recovery

The usual post-operative recovery period is four weeks. For a month after leaving the hospital, patients have frequent check-ups. Most patients are able to return to work within eight to ten weeks.[25]

The Risks of Donating a Liver

The most common complication from the surgery is bile leakage. In rare cases, a donor could die as a result of the operation (the estimated risk of dying from the transplant operation is about 1 in 500). If the remaining piece of the liver is damaged, the donor may also need a liver transplant. A donor may develop problems during or right after the operation, as well. Other risks include bleeding, infection, and damage to the bile ducts. Sometimes donors experience problems months or years after surgery. One of the most common problems is stomach pain and bulges around the scar (the bulges can usually be fixed with surgery).

Financial Cost of Donating a Liver

If they have it, the recipient's health insurance pays for the donor's health care costs, including the cost of the check-up, doctors' fees, hospital costs, and follow-up visits after surgery.

---

25. Federal employees who become organ donors are allowed a special leave period from work. Some employers have similar programs.

While costs, such as travel, lodging, loss of income from time off of work, and other related expenses (which can run into the thousands of dollars), are not usually covered by insurance, there are insurance plans that pay for some or all of these expenses.

And the worst operation footnote of all: it's common for PSC to recur in patients ten years after transplant.

* * *

After the Tufts transplant coordinator went over all of the information with us, my brother-in-law Jeff asked the coordinator, "Do you think you can get me in for some tests right now? I mean, we're here."

Jeff, too, had gone through the preliminary tests and was a blood type match. We'd been through all this with Todd and then with my mom, and I'd already found out the hard way that the odds were simply stacked against me. I appreciated Jeff's desire to do something, but sometimes, no matter how hard you fight, your number is just up. Hold your head high and try to enjoy your remaining days.

By then, I was heading downhill so fast that a somber undercurrent began running through nearly everything I did with anyone close to me. It was as if a musty old blanket had been dropped over my life. A death shroud. It wasn't so much a *Poor Bryan, he's dying and there's nothing we can do* attitude, but more that I was the object causing an unstated morose sadness to emanate from my closest friends and family whenever they were around me. Understandably so. But I hated it. Because I was still alive and my mind was very much kicking, and when that final knock came to my door, death would know I was there, because I wasn't going down without a fight. That stubborn kid—the one who had rented the ties and undercut the nuns' necktie racket and refused to wear full socks and lived for years without a door on his bedroom because of his hardheadedness—that kid was still in me, breathing like a dragon. And God help anything that would try to snuff out that boy's light. I had a *life* to live! I would not be denied.

Get up and get to work, Bryan! became a constant drumbeat in my mind. My body may have looked still and reposed many times when I was exhausted, my breathing shallow, my system racked with pain, my eyes sunken, my skin jaundiced, but *Death? Is that the **best** you can do? Doctors say I'll die soon, but you're going to have to do better than that to drag this young warhorse down.* I die when *I* say I die. Any other thought be removed from my mind.

. . . Now get up and get to work.

A couple of weeks before Christmas, I was on a working trip in Las Vegas with my friend and co-worker Matt Morrell. I shouldn't have gone on the trip, but hardheaded me . . .

We were in conferences all day and had most evenings free. After a meeting one day, Matt and I were at a restaurant for dinner when I suddenly became tired, nauseous, dizzy, and began shaking. It seemed worse than previous episodes, but I'd been to this dance a thousand times. You just grit your teeth, steel your mind and hang on. Sometimes I could wait it out and the symptoms would pass. Other times, I had to be rushed to the nearest hospital. This one was a bad episode. I was lucky to have Matt with me. It was the first time I hadn't been able to hide the extent of my illness from a coworker (and he never spoke a word about it to anyone).

Like an iron mallet on a battered bank safe, the disease was breaking through my mental toughness. My body was caving.

I could feel it. By Christmas time, I was in liver failure. Lia arranged for Todd and Melissa to pick up my dog, Lucy, and I was rushed to St. Raphael's Hospital in New Haven, in intense pain, filled with fluid, feverish, delirious.

On the way, I turned to Lia and murmured, "Do me one favor, will you? Don't give Lucy to anyone if I . . . when I . . . "

"—Stop," she cut me off, her voice choking as tears welled up in her eyes. "Don't even think those things, Bryan. This is not over."

On top of the PSC shutting my liver down, this time I was diagnosed with infection, pneumonia and ascites. Perfect recipe for a quick death.

It's true what they say: When you're at death's door, your whole life flashes before you like a movie. It was a nice picture.

I didn't want it to end.

* * *

Dear Mom & Dad,

I can't tell you how proud I am to be your son. Over the years, I have grown to appreciate the parents you are, the people you are, how you treat each other, how you treat people you know and don't know. Recently a lot of people have said a lot of nice things to me or about me and I realize the reason for this is a result of who you are and what you instilled in me. Your caring, love and involvement in my life is overwhelming for me to think of while writing this. My tears of pride and thanks speak volumes in regards to how I feel about both of you. You are both my heroes for who you are and for what you made me this day.

I love both of you from the bottom of my soul.

I love you forever,

Bryan

CHAPTER 8

Angels Among Us

Be not forgetful to entertain strangers:
for thereby some have entertained angels unawares.

—Hebrews 13:2, the Bible

Sunday, January 22, 2006

In church one Sunday in January of 2006, the priest was delivering a homily about putting one's faith and trust in God.

"When you know you have done everything you can do for a situation, let it go," he said.

My mother's attention, half on the pastor, half on the anxiety gnawing at her weary mind as she prayed desperately—for an angel, for a miracle, for *anything*—instantly riveted to his words.

"Once you've done what you can," he repeated, "give it to God."

My mom was there for comfort. She desperately needed solace, a quiet hour where she could think by herself, beseech God, hear from Him. She got what she was looking for. *I think he's talking to me*, she thought. And she gave it to God. "No one is entitled to anything," she murmured as she crossed herself and thanked God for the words of the priest. It was in God's hands now.

Just a few days earlier, she had lamented tearfully to me, "There's nothing in my power that I can do. I can't cure the disease. I can't take it out of you. I wish I could. I wish they would give it to me and we would be happy."

All that, of course, was impossible. My parents had found me the best doctors. Financially, they tried to put some money away to deal with emergencies. They left no stone unturned in doing all they could to help me, save me, protect me, be there for me. What's left to do? You give it to God and that's it. It was now out of their hands. They would be leaving the next morning.

Because an angel had appeared.

* * *

Just before Christmas of 2005, Jeff had phoned me.

"What are you doing on January 24?" he asked.

"Nothing in particular," I answered. "I just want to be around friends and family . . . you know."

"Well," he began, uncharacteristically coy, "I'm scheduled for a transplant. You want to join me?"

He explained that a few months earlier, after I'd been given the "live donor or death" ultimatum, and we'd had the family meeting with the Tufts transplant coordinator, he had secretly gone for a lab workup, X-rays and all the necessary diagnostic tests, and then signed on to be my live donor. I was stunned. He was not just my sister's husband, he was my nieces' dad. His willingness to subject himself to a dangerous operation that he didn't have to undergo and that might cost him his life (potentially creating a devastating loss for our entire family) reduced me to tears. Doctors had given Jeff three months to decide whether or not to go through with the operation.[26] He took three seconds.

Liver transplants are sometimes even more dangerous for the healthy donor than the sick recipient, and it's not uncommon for such transplants not to take. I wasn't worried about myself being cut into—I'd long before made peace with my life and was content with the eight extra years I'd been given to live after being told I only had a few months left. But Jeff didn't have to put himself in danger like this. At the very least, the procedure would leave a ragged, permanent scar on his stomach and chest.

---

26. All of the testing could have been completed in a week. But a three-month period is given to allow a potential donor time to think it through and to back out if they decide not to go through with the operation. If the donor changes their mind, the only reason the hospital would give the recipient is that the donor was found to be medically unable to proceed.

"Man, who *are* you?" I asked him as I dried my eyes after he explained everything to me. I asked him to reconsider—his wife and kids needed him. But Jeff, selfless hero that he was, was resolute. He'd made up his mind. He was giving me life.

"Who am *I*?" Jeff asked back incredulously. "It's not about me, man. Ever since I met you when we were kids, you have expressed nothing but genuine love, appreciation and affection for people. For years now, you've been living with something life threatening that you've been told you won't survive. The fact that you have used that reality to lift your thinking and behavior even higher—rather than whine or mope—and to pour encouragement into others while you face imminent death . . . Man, that indicates to me a really unusual character in this day and age."

All I could think was that we needed more people in this world like Jeff Agli to set the kind of example he was setting. And here he was trying to give me some sort of credit I didn't have coming. It was *he* who had the unusual character, selflessly stepping up and offering to literally sacrifice a necessary physical piece of his body so that I might live. *Who does that?*

Jeff had to be an angel in disguise. There was no other earthly explanation.

Jeff Agli

In the time of your life, live so that in that wondrous
time you shall not add to the misery and
sorrow of the world, but you'll smile to
the infinite delight and mystery of it.

—William Saroyan (1908–1981)

Jeff Agli was far more than father to my two nieces, Alivia and Sonia, and husband to my older sister, Kristy. Kristy herself was in a unique position, too. Her brother was dying and her husband had offered himself up for an operation that could kill him or (at the very least) would grotesquely scar him for life.

As a pediatric nurse practitioner,[27] Jeff was a thinker, an intellectual, a scientist. Long before my situation had come down to "do or die," he had begun to research my disease. Then he made a decision to step up, without consideration of personal health or safety issues. In fact, Jeff never said to Kristy, "Here's the thing I'm thinking of doing." He didn't discuss it with her. To Jeff's way of thinking, what was there to discuss? I was her brother. I was at death's door. He was a donor match. He acted.

The day Jeff called to tell me he'd secretly gone through all the testing and that the operation was scheduled for late January, Kristy was sitting in the chilly winter air on their front porch while Jeff was on the phone with me. What could a wife do but smile inside and shake her head in wonder at the fact that she had married a modern day hero. While Kristy knew the procedure could save my life, she didn't know who to be more nervous for, her husband or her brother. In her mind, she resolved that Jeff was going to be okay, but she was truly frightened about the fact that her brother was going to die if he didn't get a live transplant *real soon.*

Kristy asked Jeff, "When did you decide to do this for him?"

"When it came up last fall that he had type O Positive blood," he responded. "I thought, *Wow . . . I have type O Positive.*"

That was it. The hook was set.

---

27. A nurse practitioner specializes in work somewhat more than that of a registered nurse and less than a medical doctor, and can also prescribe medications.

Jeff worked at a hospital, so he spent a lot of time in the medical library, pulling dozens of articles, digging into PSC and live donor liver transplants, and what such operations entailed. He was initially curious to know what this thing was. To him, it was purely professional scientific curiosity, so there was no real need to discuss it with his wife. But an idea had taken root in his mind. By the time the doctors had emphatically insisted that I start looking for a live donor (or a burial plot), Jeff had already been studying up on PSC for awhile.

He also set about analyzing the practicalities of the potential donors. He and Todd were blood type matches, but in assessing who might be the better donor between them, two things weighed against Todd: he was self-employed at that time and (although he was a professional athlete and in good condition) he had a little higher cholesterol than would be considered healthy for a transplant. On the other hand, Jeff was in a little bit better shape at that point, was employed, had a great health insurance plan, and had the ability to take medical leave of absence. Those raw facts, combined with Jeff's character, sealed the deal.

"I can take time off from work and be covered," Jeff explained to Kristy. "I've read all about the danger to the donor, what I'd have to go through and all that. The one guaranteed side effect is pain. That, I can handle. The only other risk is that the liver is very vascular. Once they start to work with it, there's potential for infection."

"And potential for *death*," Kristy added bluntly.

"Your brother has been living with *that* hanging over his head every day for eight solid years," Jeff responded. He looked into his wife's eyes and added, "It's a once in a lifetime opportunity to help a person in dire need. A chance to experience something most people will never experience, feelings I would never otherwise feel."

Jeff was the type of man who liked to do things that made him feel *alive*. Climb Mt. Washington in the dead of winter when it was minus 40 degrees. Participate in Alaska's grueling Susitna 100 run across the frozen tundra. Crazy stuff like that. He often thought about what his patients must go through, what it was like from their side of the stethoscope. So, he also saw helping me in this incredible way as an opportunity to gain a better understanding of how patients who are about to undergo major surgery feel. Their worry, angst, raw fear. What it's like for a patient to awake in the hospital at three in the morning because they fell asleep at seven that evening and now can't get back to sleep. So they walk the quiet halls pushing their little wheeled pole, hearing faint beeps and labored breathing as they pass by each quiet room in the dead of night, reaching the window at the end of the corridor and looking out into the dark void beyond. The experience of living in his patients' skin. What better way to gain empathy for his charges—while helping to save his brother-in-law's life.

One of the biggest things Jeff would also gain was a better understanding of how some donors can feel afterwards. *Neglected* is not the right term, but maybe *let down*. All the hype and the fuss and focus is on the donor leading up to the operation. Everyone is amazed at their spirit of selfless altruism. They get praise, attention, thanks. And then . . . they feel almost invisible after the surgery is over, because while they're recovering in bed, everyone is focused on the recipient, no longer on the donor— they assume the donor is healthy now, just like when they came into the hospital.

Jeff was told that after the operation he was going to be in more pain than I was,[28] because I would be going from a liver that didn't function to a liver that was working wonderfully. But Jeff was the kind of man who accepted that there was simply going to be pain in these types of experiences, so bring on the pain and get it over with. Bryan would be better for the experience, and Jeff could notch another experience in his ongoing quest to help people. He was on the bone marrow list. He donated blood. Now he would be adding "liver donor" to the list.

All Kristy could do would be to minimize in her mind any potential negative effects to her husband and to her brother . . . and hang on for the ride.

* * *

A man's character is his fate.

—Heraclitus (540–480 B.C.), *On the Universe*

When my dad asked Jeff's mother, Judy, how she felt about the decision Jeff had made, she answered with no hesitation: "I'd expect nothing less."

Jeff Agli was raised in Connecticut in a beautiful town named Branford, three houses from the ocean in a home willed to his grandfather, who sold it to Jeff's parents for one dollar. They took out a small mortgage and winterized the house, and there he and his sister were raised.

---

28. When more than half of the liver is taken, they can't give the donor as much pain medicine as they normally would, because the liver metabolizes most of the medication. So the donor is also being shortchanged on pain meds and guaranteed to be extremely uncomfortable.

Jeff would describe his family as "pretty dysfunctional." His dad (a professor at a local university) was focused mostly on himself and wasn't at all positive, loving or encouraging toward Jeff, his mother and his sister. His dad never told him he was proud of him, never gave him positive encouragement. Everything was delivered from a negative standpoint. Jeff was verbally beaten down. He was always made to feel not quite good enough. He was constantly told he didn't do things quite the best way. There was no physical abuse, just a steady drumbeat of emotional, mental and verbal derision that can take a toll on a kid. It wasn't until he was fourteen and his parents were getting a divorce that Jeff realized that his dad's "method" of raising healthy, well-balanced kids in preparation for living a well-rounded, productive life was not working. Jeff's mother, an extremely caring and generous woman, would say that she probably stayed married to the man for a bit too long.

In his senior year in high-school, Jeff played three sports, was in the high-school musical, and was also in the National Honor Society. He was what most kids probably dream of being. He was smart, talented, athletic. Jeff had his mother's genes through and through. They were good people.

The person I had turned out to be by then was reflective of my parents, my upbringing, and the way my father drilled into me the proper way to behave. Jeff, on the other hand, was self-made—completely unique. You could never recreate a man like him, regardless of what a parent or a childhood brought to the equation. Something about Jeff was just . . . special.

It may have been fate that I met Jeff long before he even knew I had a sister named Kristy, and that she would someday become his wife and bear his children. I first met him through a childhood friend of mine whose family owned a summer house near Jeff's home. Many years later, in 1999, when he pulled into our driveway to pick up my sister, fate was only halfway toward revealing that just seven years after that surprise appearance as my sister's date, Jeff would be giving me more than half of his liver to save my life.

Jeff and Kristy met in April of 1999 when he was in grad school. Thirteen months later, they were married and she was pregnant. My dad basically became the father Jeff never really had, and the Donahues became the family he'd always wanted. At some point in all that activity, Jeff's attitude about life and career and love began to skyrocket. By then, I had PSC and was struggling to maintain a positive outlook. Jeff's buoyancy along the way took my mind off of one big worry: my sister and nieces couldn't be in better hands.

Being raised by a man who didn't do his job as a dad was a perfect model for Jeff on how *not* to be a dad. If men tended toward machismo, kept everything in and rarely talked about how they felt, then Jeff would make sure he didn't become that way. He even went so far as to ignore gender stereotyping and chose a profession that some people still think of as a non-male job: nursing. He brought to his profession a demeanor that was gentle and approachable, yet disciplined and masculine.[29]

Jeff had always wanted to work in health care. Originally, he worked with adults, in cardiac rehabilitation. But trying to get adults to change fifty-year habits proved to be an uphill battle. Children were more disciplined than that crowd. When he volunteered at a camp for children with terminal illnesses, he knew immediately what he wanted to do. He hadn't felt much

---

29. Bolstering his image as a nurse were Jeff's rugged, anti-hero looks. He could pass as a young version of the modern cowboy played by Kirk Douglas in the movie *Lonely Are The Brave*.

self-worth when he was growing up, so he knew how life could beat a kid down. He had learned firsthand that kids just want love and encouragement; they flourish under it. Jeff loved children, he liked being challenged and was intrigued with the idea of having to have feelings and emotions—which you're going to have around kids who are under duress, whether you're trying to pump them up or calm them down. Finally finding what he wanted to do in life made Jeff flourish. He soon became a pediatric nurse practitioner at a children's hospital.

"Kids are the best patients ever," Jeff once told me. "With an adult, you poke them with a needle and they get mad at you. But kids—even though they cry—as they're walking away crying, they *thank you!* It's unbelievably rewarding. Read some obituaries of kids I've worked with, and when you see all the things they went through when they were alive, you realize that sometimes we adults need to learn to just suck it up. Our travails are nothing compared to what many children suffer."

He had found his passion: Learning from children how to love unconditionally. His credo for life became a phrase from a Forest Witcraft poem called *Within My Power*:

> "One hundred years from now, it will not matter what kind of car I drove, what kind of house I lived in, how much was in my bank account, nor what my clothes looked like. But the world may be a better place because I was important in the life of a child."

* * *

*Courage is not the absence of fear but rather
the judgment that something else is more
important than fear.*

—Ambrose Redmoon

Sunday, January 22, 2006, would be my last opportunity to say some good-byes before Jeff and I left for the hospital early the following morning.

My younger sister, Amy, and her husband, Adam, had a newborn baby (Grace) and wouldn't be able to go with us to Boston. I had always deliberately kept Amy from the full truth about my condition. It would be tough to tell her goodbye.

Lia and I stopped by to see them before going to the hospital.

"Until you actually had to have this transplant," Amy told me, "it was almost not real to me. It makes life so very valuable, knowing that it could be gone so suddenly, at such a young age."

I told her I had written a letter to her, but that I didn't want her to read it unless the transplant was unsuccessful. She said that she would keep the letter wherever she went, that it would be a reminder not to sweat the small stuff with the special-needs children she taught.

I didn't want to start crying in front of my little sister, so I handed her the envelope containing the letter, and Lia and I left.

Dear Amy, Adam and Grace,

Over the last few years I have struggled with the thought that Amy is my younger sister and I am supposed to take care of her. Not to my liking, the tides were turned and she has taken care of me.

113

I can't thank Adam enough for who he is and the way he takes care of you Amy.

Amy, as far back as I can remember, you have always been a great person, sister and friend. You have grown into a remarkable person, lady, wife and now mother. While I am writing this, I am crying. My tears are not from sadness, but out of pride and thanks. I am proud that I can stand beside the three of you and call you my family. The feelings I have for you guys and the place in my heart can't find their way to the tip of my pen, but never forget they are there.

I hope that when you are around me you feel and know how much I love all three of you. I am truly blessed by God to have you in my life.

Smile toward the future, and know that I love you.

Bryan

* * *

As Lia and I drove away from Amy's house, I thought of my longtime friend Todd. On October 30, 1989, my cousin Melissa had met Todd at a little league baseball game when they were in secondary school. Todd had been a part of the Donahue clan for so long that I thought of him as more of a brother than a friend—long before he and Melissa had gotten married.

It was just a decade ago, in 1996, that Todd's sister Leah had been killed by a drunk driver. Half of Todd's family was in the car, his youngest sister and brother, and his sister's friend, dozing on the way home after a long afternoon at a hockey game, on their way to drop off Todd's grandfather. Todd's dad had been driving. To go home, they could turn right and go through town, or go left and drive by the ocean. Todd's dad chose the beach. Quieter, more picturesque . . . and the same route that led them to the drunk driver who had just sped through a red light.

Leah was fourteen. She was the only one to die.

Todd's father took it the worst. He replayed his innocent decision in his mind over and over and over. It tore at him for years.

I remembered vividly the day Leah died. She was a freshman at Sacred Heart Academy. When I heard the news, I was in utter disbelief. A hole of sadness filled my heart. At the wake, Todd's father just sat there, not moving a muscle as his little girl lay in her school uniform. I hugged Todd and didn't want to let go. I was comforted by him hugging me, but I didn't know what to say. Then I understood his dad's silence. There are no words when your world is suddenly wrenched from beneath you.

Several years later, during Todd's first year as a fireman, his unit was dispatched to a fatal car accident on the highway near his station. His truck was the first one on the scene. By then, Todd had been trained to view such tragedies with a professional detachment that would allow him to quickly assess the damage. He approached the wreck, thinking, *Somebody's got to identify this body* . . . and then he saw the body. A mangled girl of twenty-two. And his mind ripped him back to the fatal night his little sister, Leah, had been taken in the same gruesome manner. Leah would have been only a couple of years older than this girl, had she lived.

The biggest impact his sister's death had on Todd (especially after he became a fireman) was that it drove home how death was a daily part of life and could take any of us at any time.

Less than twenty-four months after Leah's funeral, I would again be stunned to silence, in a doctor's office in Boston, after being told I had only months to live.

If you think you have problems, just put them on the table in comparison to everyone else's, and I guarantee you'll take yours back.

—Bob Donahue

* * *

The mood was somber on the way to Boston. Nobody spoke. Just nervous quips now and then as the dismal cold drifted past us outside the car. I tried to keep my mind off of what Jeff and I would be facing in less than twenty-four hours.

I reflected back on all the times we had made mad dashes over this same highway over the years. Like firemen down the brass pole at the first blare of the alarm, we'd become old hands at getting out of the house and on the road in minutes each time a near-death flare-up of PSC threatened my life. My first such run, back in September of 1999, taught us the hard way the importance of being prepared in advance, of knowing where everything was and what to do if things got off track. We learned to keep overnight bags packed and ready to go, car gassed up at all times, cash in the house (because if I suddenly became ill and needed to get to Boston immediately, they didn't want to have to divert to an ATM).

Like anyone who suddenly faces major health catastrophes, you are shocked—you never thought it could happen to you. And when it does happen, you don't really believe it is happening, so you don't know how to prepare in the midst of the sudden emergency because you simply don't know what to expect. My mom and dad had come up with a plan. Since my dad was on the road a lot for his work and his office was halfway between our house and Boston, they chose a designated commuter parking lot where they would meet if they needed to get me quickly to the Tufts New England Medical Center in Boston. The plan was that my mom would call my dad and tell him I was sick and needed to get to Tufts, she would meet him at the lot and together they would rush me to the hospital. They had a list of all the hotels in a certain radius of Tufts, phone numbers ready, cash in hand, Visa card with a clear balance so they could always use it. They had learned that the hard way, slept in enough sleazy places.

One time there was a computer software convention going on in Boston, which meant that everyone in the world had converged on the city. It was late at night and we couldn't find any available rooms anywhere, so my mom and Lia had to stay at a "no-tell motel" that charged by the hour. They slept on top of the blankets, fully clothed, T-shirt over the pillowcases. They were desperate and just needed a place to lie down for the night while I was being operated on. Part of the problem was that emergencies like mine weren't something for which you could plan ahead. All of a sudden, I was violently ill and we had to *go*. You can't always get reservations on such short notice. You just get on the road, run down your list and hope for the best, knowing you'd prepared all you could for these things.[30] We learned the hard way in those early days the importance of trying to make things easier on us all.

---

30. Yet, even though we lived less than four miles from Yale, we couldn't even imagine going anywhere but Tufts New England Medical Center in Boston. They were that good—the staff, support group, doctors, everyone.

And now, after more than five years of rushing to the world famous Tufts, I was making what I hoped would be my last run.

* * *

We arrived grimfaced at Tufts New England Medical Center around two in the afternoon on Monday, January 23, 2006, and trudged the corridors to meet with Dr. Rohrer, the lead surgeon. As we walked, I thought about all I'd been through the past few years, when a young child was suddenly wheeled by us with tubes going in everywhere, no hair, gaunt little face. As the years had gone by and I had managed to stay alive, I felt blessed to have had the extra time I'd had. You gain a deep appreciation for life when you realize that there are little children who are having a rougher time of it and who might never enjoy as many years living as I had avoiding dying.

By ten that night, Jeff and I were each in our rooms. I was trying unsuccessfully to sleep. Jeff was reading a letter . . .

> *Dear Jeff,*
>
> *This is the epitome of the expression "Words cannot express the way I feel."*
>
> *I know you are truly doing this out of just pure goodness and do not expect even a thank you or to be thought of as a hero, but I hope you know how much we appreciate you giving us another chance at life.*
>
> *I know you've been told, but if I think of someone who's considered a "hero," I think of someone who is selfless, kind, and saves lives*

just because. You truly fit that definition. You are an inspiration and the type of person we should all aspire to be like.

I wish I could take on all of yours and Bryan's pain and stress that comes with this surgery so you would not have to endure what you are about to go through.

*Jeff, we will **never** be able to show our appreciation for all that you have done and are doing. I wish you a speedy recovery as I cheer you on "The Amazing Race"*

Thank you! Thank you! Thank you!

Love always,

Lia

Tuesday, January 24, 2006

In the pre-dawn hours of January 24, 2006, I had one of the most powerful conversations I'd had ever had in my life. It was seven words long and it took place during the two minutes just before Jeff was taken into surgery . . .

"I love you," I told him.

"I love you back," he smiled. When Jeff Agli smiles, there is something in his eyes, something indefinable, something knowing, like he knows something special that most people don't, cosmic things, secret things. It's just a look.

Then he was wheeled to surgery. And I broke down and cried like a baby.

I was in the operating room by 7:30 a.m. They would operate on Jeff first, to make sure they could safely remove the part of his liver that I needed and be reasonably assured that he could survive the operation. Once they determined that the operation could go forward, they would extract my piece of his liver, leaving less of his liver in him than they were putting into me.[31]

During the surgeries, my mom and dad, Lia and her parents, and Jeff's mom and Kristy waited in the hospital's family room. Time ground to a nail-biting crawl. Jeff's surgery, they said, would take six hours. I would be in for twelve. After several hours of waiting, Kristy couldn't take anymore. It was two in the afternoon when Kristy stepped out of the family room to walk off her anxiety and ran into Dr. Freeman on his way to talk to us.

"How are they doing?" Kristy asked nervously as they entered the family room.

"Jeff is in recovery," he announced. "His surgery was successful." The room erupted in tears of relief. "We were able to remove the necessary piece of his liver, and we're almost halfway through Bryan's surgery."

He told Kristy she would be able to visit her husband in an hour. Hearing that Jeff had come through the operation without complications took much of the heaviness off of everyone's shoulders. Although Jeff still faced many weeks of recovery time, at least his body seemed to be handling the surgery. Dr. Freeman went on to explain that as soon as they had inserted Jeff's liver into me, my body reacted well and began immediately pumping bile. But it would be a few more hours than anticipated until my surgery was complete, because my diseased liver was worse than expected; it had taken a few extra hours just to remove it.

While the good news of Jeff's successful operation was a much needed break from the awful tension, they still had a long time

---

31. They would transplant 60 percent (2.2 pounds) of his liver into me. After the transplant, both livers soon grow to full size in the recipient and the donor, usually within a few weeks (though sometimes, it can take up to several months).

to endure until my surgery would be finished. Tension ratcheted back up after Dr. Freeman left to go back to the operating room. As they waited, they scrutinized every person who happened past the doorway. A couple of hours later, Dr. Cooper, one of the transplant surgeons involved in both surgeries, entered the room.

"It's going well, but it's going to take some time," he said. He explained that they were taking a vein from my leg to connect to my new liver, and making other connections to help blood flow.

Lia and my parents tried to decipher warning signs in what he was saying, but Dr. Cooper didn't seem unduly concerned.

At eight that evening, more than twelve hours after I entered surgery, Dr. Rohrer appeared. By then, my family was ragged from exhausted, stress and worry.

"It's over," Dr. Rohrer announced. "It was a success."

Sobs of joy burst from Lia and my mom.

It was another hour or two after the transplant before Lia and my parents were allowed to see me. The surgery intensive care unit looked like something from a NASA spacecraft. I was hooked up to every conceivable machine, intubated, out cold, strapped down, a line in my neck, a tube in my nose, several IVs and arterial lines going in and out, fluid bags hanging everywhere, three or four drains coming out of my stapled abdomen. The joy that had swept over everyone just before they were led into the recovery room instantly faded as they saw the fragile state I was in. Doctors explained that I had sustained nerve damage during surgery and had lost much of the function of my left arm.

But I was alive. After twelve hours of being sliced and diced, and after eight grueling years of living constantly on the doorstep of death, I had a whole new life ahead of me. I had won.

* * *

A few days after his operation, Jeff was able to put on a sweat-shirt (to cover the drains and other lines sticking out of him) and shuffle to the family room to see Alivia, Sonia and Kristy. Kristy had held up incredibly well throughout the entire ordeal. Here was a woman who'd had both her brother and her husband in the hospital for major surgery and two little children to keep calm and distracted while their daddy and Uncle Bubbie were being carved into. Kristy endured it all with an upbeat grace that made me proud to be her brother.

After keeping her emotions in check during her long ordeal, she could finally allow herself to cry.

> *Dear Kristy, Jeff, Alivia and Sonia,*
>
> *For the last 29 years I have felt that I am the luckiest person on earth. Kristy, as your younger brother, I admire you for the person you are and have always been. I regret the fact that until this day I never told you how much I have looked up to you. You are an outstanding person who I love beyond belief. When I sit down alone, my chest hurts because of the joy and pride you give me when I think back on our childhood and where we have come to today. You are an extraordinary mother of two beautiful girls that bring so much joy to my life. I have to fight back tears of joy and pride. I can't thank Jeff enough for the way he treats you and loves you.*

Smile toward the future and know I love you,

Bryan

The Light at the End of the Tunnel

The day after surgery, Jeff was still in recovery and I was still in the ICU. By late morning, he was able to sit in a chair and visit with Kristy.

That afternoon, I was awake, my breathing tube removed, and I was able to talk to Lia.

That evening, Jeff was able to take a wheelchair stroll down the corridor with the assistance of nurses.

The third day after surgery, my liver test scores were already showing marked improvement—even though I was experiencing pain in my left arm, had lost twenty pounds and had shed a liter of fluid since that Monday. I was helped to Jeff's room. He was still in a tremendous amount of pain. *Hero* doesn't begin to describe what he was going through for me.

The next day, I was fairly stable and Jeff's pain had subsided. He managed a grin and asked me, "How's my liver doing?"

"Great," I smiled back. "How's it feel being the amazing two-livered superhero?"

By Sunday, Jeff and I both were able to walk the floor and visit each other. He'd also started his liquid diet and had his IV tubes taken out. His patience at being on the soft side of a hospital bed was wearing thin. As a nurse practitioner, he preferred to be giving medical attention, rather than receiving it.

By the morning of January 31, Jeff was up and about and raring to go home. He'd be released the following day and would be home by early afternoon.

On the afternoon of Friday, February 3, I was released. It was finally over.

It was as if the surgeons had opened up the hood and given me a brand new engine.

—Chris Klug, Olympic Medallist[32]

It was wonderful to be home (once again!), to have my face licked by my dog, Lucy, to wake up in my own bed next to my wife. I could feel new life coursing through my system almost immediately after getting Jeff's liver in me. I was instructed to go to Boston every week for follow-ups and have lab work done locally three times per week. My appetite quickly returned and I soon began to feel like my old self again.

When I had come home from the hospital, I'd discovered that Kelly McGuinness had hired a cleaning crew for my family and for Jeff's family (for six whole months!). And every day for a few weeks after my operation, Kelly came over and brought or made lunch for me and whoever was visiting me. Talk about winning the employment lotto all over again. How many people could brag that their boss schlepped them and their pals meals in bed? I could get used to this.

On Monday, February 6, almost two weeks after the operations, Jeff and I went to Boston for a post-op checkup and ongoing tests. Jeff had been experiencing some severe pain. I was in pain myself. The roundtrip was rough for both of us.

The next evening, doctors asked me to go back to the hospital on the following day for more tests. Lia and I drove to Boston that

---

32. Chris Klug, *To The Edge And Back: My Story from Organ Transplant Survivor to Olympic Snowboarder* (Carroll & Graf Publishers, 2004), p.240.

night. But that same day, Jeff had developed a fever, and he and Kristy decided to drive to Boston, as well.

I was admitted that morning before Jeff arrived. After running some tests on me, doctors announced that my stats were elevated and they wanted to keep an eye on me. They also decided to admit Jeff, so they could try to discover the cause of his fever. Doctors weren't particularly alarmed for either of us. We were experiencing fairly routine physical responses to having a major organ cut out of one person and implanted into another.

I was released at noon the next day. Jeff stayed until his fever broke, and was released that Saturday. His fever hadn't fully subsided, but he'd grumbled and ranted so much that after agreeing to phone his temperatures in to the doctor, they booted him out. He was finally back with his girls.

By the fourth week after the operation, Jeff was on his way back to his normal self, walking two miles per day; and I wasn't doing too badly myself.

By March, all tests were good and I was finally out of the woods. By then, I had gained a new universe of appreciation for the term *friends*. Life was good! I was happy. Finally, I could relax, pursue my dreams, and lavish love, appreciation and attention on Lia. Although she claimed that it all came with the territory, I owed my successful recovery to her. She had been holding down the fort, going to work, taking care of me (*putting up* with me!), and was by my side and ahead of my thoughts the entire time. She made being a new man feel beyond wonderful. She was my reason to live. And I was finally doing just that.

I thought of Chris Klug, the professional snowboarder from Vail, Colorado. Klug had begun snowboarding in the early 1980s, eventually going on to win four World Cup races, three Grand

Prix races, five National titles, the U.S. Open and—the same year I was diagnosed with PSC—a sixth place certificate in the 1998 Nagano Winter Olympics. And the entire time Chris was racing in those Olympic Games in Japan, he too had PSC.[33]

In Denver in early 1995 at University Hospital, Klug had been diagnosed with the same disease I'd had all those years. He was just twenty-three when he was diagnosed. He was put on the liver transplant waiting list, and over the next few years was given the medication treatments and went through regular ERCP procedures to drain the bile buildup, just like me. He continued to race—while keeping his illness a secret. That is, until 2000, when the disease took a turn for the worse. That May, Chris was moved quickly up the donor list. If he didn't get a new liver, they told him, he would die. Ninety days later, on July 27, 2000, he got the call and was rushed in for a liver transplant in Denver. He was out of the hospital in four days, took just one month to recover and was snowboarding by that September. By the end of that year, it was his most successful season ever as a professional athlete. In fact, less than two years later, in the 2002 Winter Olympic Games, he took home a bronze medal.

If Chris Klug could fight a battle with PSC and come out on top, then why not me?

Just six weeks after my transplant, I asked myself that very question. Because that's when it all came crashing down.

---

33. Chris Klug, *To The Edge And Back: My Story from Organ Transplant Survivor to Olympic Snowboarder* (Carroll & Graf Publishers, 2004).

CHAPTER 9

In a Heartbeat

Nobody is entitled to anything—there's no entitlement out there in this world. You have to work for it, earn it . . . or get it by the grace of God.

—Milly Donahue

I had been making progress, but I wasn't out of the woods. As February of 2006 had drawn to a close, after being in and out of the hospital with an infection, I was having blood drawn and tested several times per week. I still had staples and drains in me, was on medication and was weak and sore from the surgery. That was all fairly routine after major transplant surgery.

On Sunday, March 5, Lia and I decided to take a walk so I could begin rebuilding my stamina. It was time to get out into the chilly spring air and start getting myself back into shape. My goal was to eventually get close to the physical condition I was in while in the Marine Corps. I knew it would take awhile; I'd just start light and slowly build up. But suddenly, after less than a quarter of a mile, I doubled over with a stomach cramp so severe that I struggled to get back home.

Lia had a baby shower to go to later that day. I assured her I would be okay, that I had probably just overestimated my readiness to start exercising. Lia called my mom to come over while I called Tufts for advice on the pain. They told me to call back if it got worse, or if I became feverish. It did. The pain became so excruciating that I felt like I was dying. My mom called Lia. I called the hospital. They said it was probably another infection and told me to leave immediately, a room would be ready for me. Lia rushed home and grabbed our emergency travel kit and bags. Just as she was about to shut off the bedroom lights, they gave an odd flicker—a premonition we were familiar with. We raced to Boston.

If you ever want to get fast, first class service at a hospital, forget the emergency room—walk in the front door and collapse.

129

We pulled up to the front of the hospital, bypassed the ER, and headed straight to Admitting. I hit the floor in a dead faint and was instantly swarmed by orderlies and nurses. They instructed us to get over to the ER, but I couldn't move. My mom arrived and Lia ran in search of a wheelchair. They got me into a room on the Four North Floor and a team immediately began running a battery of tests on me. I thought I was either dying or would have to have another transplant.

"Can you stand?" a nurse asked.

"Yes," I mumbled weakly, my heart thumping out of my chest. I started to rise—and immediately became dizzy and collapsed again.

When I came to, I was in such unbearable pain that I asked the nurse not to keep me alive. They wheeled me down for a CAT scan. While getting onto the table, I vomited and passed out. The scan indicated that there was nothing wrong inside me, confirming for them that it was probably another infection.

Even professionals sometimes make big mistakes.

They got me back to my room and left me a urine sample cup. As I stepped toward the bathroom, I passed out again. Lia (who is very petite) caught me and tried to get me onto the bed, but I was dead weight.

"Nurse! *Nurse!*" she cried out. No one heard her.

She finally managed to drag me up enough to get me onto the bed and ran into the hall.

"Nurse!" she screamed, in tears.

Nurses rushed in, took my blood pressure.

"Forty-eight over twenty-six," one called out.

"*What?* The CAT scan said he's okay!"

When your blood pressure is forty-eight over twenty-six, you are below comatose and barely above dead. They were baffled.

Infections don't generally reduce blood pressure—not to such alarming levels. They gave me a sedative. I passed out.

A cot had been set up in the room for Lia. That night, she dozed fitfully, waking abruptly every so often to make sure my chest was rising and falling. Early the next morning, the nurse coordinator for the transplant team came in and reviewed my charts and lab reports. She became increasingly distraught as she read through the file. Then she abruptly rushed out and returned minutes later with the transplant surgeon, a man who was usually very pleasant and upbeat. This time, his demeanor was somber as he analyzed the CAT scan and checked my vitals.

Suddenly, he dropped everything and yelled, "We're taking him in—*NOW*," and began yanking cords and calling out orders.

He wheeled my bed out of the room and into the elevator, where another doctor jumped on me and sliced my neck with a scalpel. "Sorry about this," he apologized tersely as he ran a central line into me. There was no time for anesthetic.

I'd been suffering profuse internal bleeding; they removed two pints of blood. During the surgery, Lia and my mom were in the hallway in tears that I had been basically bleeding out since the previous day, my insides pooling with blood.

Several anguished hours after my dad arrived, the surgeon wearily strode into the family room and slumped onto the couch next to Lia.

"He lost a lot of blood from the internal bleeding," he said. He was distraught at how much time had been lost from the misreading of the CAT scan the previous day. "We gave him a blood transfusion," he continued. "And he'll need another one." He paused and let out a labored sigh, then added, "The bleeding has stopped. But we weren't able to find the source." He said they hoped that it had somehow scarred itself off and wouldn't start

131

back up. "If it does," he said grimly, "we'll have to put him back on the donor list." And they would have to perform the transplant all over again, this time with a cadaver liver. If one could be found quickly enough.

Lia and my parents were stunned. To have come so far after going through so much, and now to be facing the prospect that I might have to repeat it all again was devastating. After all Jeff had endured, I had endured, our families and loved ones had endured. The same nightmare all over again. Jeff had sacrificed his life and health for nothing. And there was no assurance that I would get another liver before it was too late.

In the intensive care unit, I was so delirious that I thought the big machine in the room was a fireplace with people hiding behind it, and that the fastest way to get a nurse into ICU was to start yanking lines out of me. They put me to sleep and tied my arms down.

I was not dying easy.

There was nothing in the world that could have prepared Lia and my parents for how bad it had all turned. I had been doing fine, my new liver seemed to be functioning well for weeks, and suddenly my skin was yellow again and I was back in intensive care. The celebration of my healing had ended almost as abruptly as it had begun just a handful of weeks earlier. Lia and my parents had so quickly gone from a stadium cheer of excitement and elation that I'd made it past the transplant, to now feeling completely defeated and thinking I was literally dying before their eyes.

Lia had to update the family, but she was so stunned and numb that she couldn't. What could she write? "Bryan looks horrible"?

She called my friend Todd and said, "I just wanted you to know that I saw Bryan and . . ." she stopped, struggling to maintain her composure.

". . . And what, Lia?" Todd prompted.

She began to choke up. "I'm going to bed," she said.

"What happened?" Todd pressed in alarm.

How could she even begin to tell him I looked like a cadaver.

"Lia, what's wrong?" Todd repeated.

"He . . . he just doesn't look good. They tell me he's fine but . . ." She stopped talking, not wanting anyone else to be upset, convinced it was my last day.

* * *

Just before my liver transplant operation a few months earlier, I had made a decision to close ranks, asking Lia not to reveal any details of what I was going through during my hospital stay. In keeping with my mindset that our mental attitude and the way we choose to look at and respond to challenges in life determines the path of our life, I didn't want her to write in the hospital "Facebook" care pages (which were open to everybody) things like, "Bryan feels pretty bad today," or, "Things aren't going well." Instead, I wanted the update messages to involve only bare bones information or positive results, such as, "He's alive," "We're still here," or, "He might be going home in five days." Nothing deep, nothing negative. I wanted only a small handful of people closest to me personally to know the full details. I had no desire to tell the world how badly things were actually going. I guarded information closely during those dark days. I had a battle to focus on, and that battle began and ended in my own mind. I needed a virtual cocoon of powerful, positive mental energy to fight and win this war. I was circling the wagons, in raw survival mode, *mano a mano* with death. In situations like these, you have to take care of yourself first in order to be able to be there for others.

I didn't want a pity party standing around my bed, didn't want people feeling sorry for me or bad for themselves because of my situation.

So Lia kept my care pages updates sparse. All the peripheral melodrama remained strictly between me and a tiny handful of trusted people, who were asked not to share what was going on with me, especially in my most critical stages. I kept my turmoil, pain and struggles private. I even gave Lia a list of people who weren't allowed to come visit me. What I was going through was so enormous that I needed to feel completely comfortable knowing that information about me would stay private, and would be used only for positive purposes, with no spin, no negative, no drama. When you're dying, you do whatever you feel is necessary to beat death.

During the original operation, Lia had been keeping my boss and close friend Kelly McGuinness updated, from my transplant through my hospital recovery. It was a major thing for Kelly to drive to Boston and back, taking a full day of out of her work schedule for the five hour round trip on the road, so I assured her that it would be easier on my mind if Lia would just keep her posted on a regular basis. Kelly understood that it was crucial to keep all but my wife and parents away during surgeries so my focus would not be distracted by worried people hovering in the waiting room during my operations. So Kelly had remained at the ready, waiting for Lia's updates. Now, five weeks later, with my situation far worse, all bets were off. It was time to call her in.

* * *

As I was being taken into surgery, I mumbled to Lia, "Is Kelly coming? Did you talk to her?"

Lia was surprised at my request, not wanting to tell me *no*, not wanting to alarm Kelly with an odd request that she come while I was in surgery . . . and not wanting to face what my request probably meant. But now, at the apex of pain and convinced I was at death's door, it was time to call Kelly.

Lia phoned and asked her, "Are you coming?"

"What's going on—is he okay?" Kelly replied.

"He's asking for you." It was all Lia could say.

"*What?*" Kelly responded, immediately concerned. She knew that my "stay away" edict didn't apply to her. And she also knew how bad things must be if I was breaking my rule and asking her to come.

"He's asking for you, Kelly," Lia repeated quietly.

"I'm leaving now," Kelly replied.

Kelly made the two hour and fifteen minute drive to Boston in ninety minutes. When she arrived in the waiting room, my mom burst into tears and fell into her arms.

"I don't think he's going to make it," my mother sobbed.

Lia came out to get Kelly and they entered the intensive care unit, where I looked as if I were at death's door.

The next thing I knew, I awoke in the surgery intensive care unit, with Lia, my parents and Kelly McGuinness staring down at me.

"You've been fighting this for eight years," Kelly said, her eyes drilling into mine. "You have no right to give up—not now. You're the only one who can decide what your outcome is going to be."

Kelly had come in with such a bold positiveness that it virtually proclaimed *This is **not** the end*, that I was going to make it through. Her presence almost immediately changed the mood and the spirit in the room. And that's exactly what my survival called for. The mere fact that she was there steeled my mind into *knowing* that now was not my time to go. I had to keep fighting. I couldn't give up. The positive mental psychological authority Kelly exuded was palpable (and not just to me, but to others around her). She practically materialized reality. *You are **not** to die!* Not today.

That night, Kelly drove back home, and Lia and my parents returned to their hotel room.[34]

"Do you want me to stay with you?" my mother asked Lia.

"No, I'll be okay," Lia answered.

That night, as she finally began to drift to sleep, Lia leaned over to shut off the bedside lamp. When she turned the switch, it sparked off . . . and then mysteriously turned itself back on. She recalled the same flickering in our bedroom light when we had left for Boston earlier. This time, the same odd occurrence happened five more times. She turned it off, it sparked, then turned itself back on. After the high emotions of the day, Lia became frightened. *There's a ghost in this room*, she thought . . . . Bryan's ghost.

In full panic, she called my mom and asked her to come to her room. My mom ran in.

"I think it's Nonni," Mom said after Lia explained what had happened.

My grandmother "Nonni" had passed away a few years earlier. Though she lived in Florida, she somehow always knew when I was sick. If we fudged and told her I was fine, she would call us on it. "I know you're lying," she'd admonish us sternly. She knew right away when I had gotten home from the hospital after being there for a few days. We would walk in the door and the phone would

---

34. Kelly went home that night, and the next day she drove all the way back again. That second day, she lifted me even more. Two days in a row she came to the hospital; nearly ten hours of driving.

immediately start ringing—and it would be her. Somehow, Nonni always knew.

"I think Nonni's telling you everything's going to be alright," my mom told Lia reassuringly.

The conjecture put Lia at ease. Mom went back to her room. When Lia turned off the light, it stayed off. Nonni had spoken. Everything was going to be okay.

On March 10, after five days in intensive care, I was released from the ICU and put into a room. By the 13th, I was up and walking around. And on March 15, I went home.

They never did locate the source of the bleeding, but it stopped.

And at long last, all was well . . . . Or so we thought.

Not *Again!*

> *Dé-jà vu [F., Déjà vu, adj., already seen]:*
> *"Something overly or unpleasantly familiar."*
>
> —Webster's New Collegiate Dictionary

Unbelievably, in June of 2006, after a great couple of months back at work, my *original symptoms* all returned. Fatigue, jaundice, pain—everything that had been caused by the PSC blockage to the common bile duct—all over again. *What was going on!?* Raw panic and dark memories flooded my mind. Death, it seemed, would simply not be denied Bryan Donahue, not after being thwarted for so long—twice in the past five months alone.

I was rushed back to the hospital, where they discovered that scar tissue had built up around my common bile duct. For two consecutive weeks, they pushed a wire through my ribs and into my liver to try to poke holes in the scar tissue. It was an operation for which I was required to be awake the entire time. The effort was unsuccessful.

Dr. Freeman, my transplant physician, came in and sat on my bed.

"You have two options," he stated bluntly. "You can have a port with a tube and a bag installed permanently on your side that bile would flow into regularly. Or you can have surgery, where we go in from both sides and try to unblock the duct." He hesitated a moment, then added, "That method is not that common."

"How uncommon is it?" I asked.

"I read of one other attempt at it before."

"Only *one?*"

Yet again in my short life, I had an impossible choice to make. This time it was either wear a bile drain bag until I die, or undergo a rare, new and radical surgery procedure to try to fix the problem. I asked myself the usual question: *What have I got to lose?*

They scheduled the surgery.

When I got into the operating room, there were several different surgical teams, in case something went wrong.

I appreciated the fact that Dr. Freeman had told me the plain, unvarnished truth. He didn't make excuses, didn't say what I wanted to hear, didn't give me platitudes or try to pacify me. He simply set my expectations and then put his skill and experience to work.

When the operation was over, Dr. Freeman expressed surprise and elation that it had been a success. It could have gone either way.

* * *

By now, barely out of my twenties, I had repeatedly escaped the jaws of death and proven myself impossible to keep down. Hopefully, death would leave me alone for a few decades.

I went back to work a few weeks after that final operation and experienced my most productive month of work ever. How was that possible? The difference was my *outlook*. Before all of these operations and procedures I was going through, I had made a consistent effort to make every day a good day. But now, they were all *great* days, because I was not supposed to be alive—*if* I had accepted the dire diagnoses of my imminent death.

Through my eight-year ordeal, I gained a deep appreciation for life. It was a reminder of two important things: Never forget what you have (because what you thought you had could be gone in a heartbeat); and love people always, unconditionally, no matter what (because any of us could be gone in a heartbeat).

With the nightmare finally over, my new life could at last begin. This time, for *real*.

I sat down and wrote the most important letter I had ever written . . .

> *Dear Lia,*
>
> *Hearing your voice, seeing your face, feeling the love you have for me, is more powerful than anything I have ever believed existed. Every day I wake up, I aspire to be more like you. Your positive outlook, your larger than life heart and your love for me are unspeakable and overwhelming. It is not often that people are given a second chance at life with time to reflect back on the past to change the future. I am making a promise*

to you and to myself, starting with this letter, to live each day with your heart and outlook.

I can't put into words how much I love you, and how proud I am that I am your husband. I am honored, blessed and humbled to be a part of your life. On a daily basis we say "I love you" to each other. The words are great, but the feeling is out of this world. Just knowing how much I am loved by you puts any struggle out of my mind. Lia, you calm and comfort me. My ultimate desire on this earth is for you to know and more importantly feel how much love I have for you. Not only have you stood me up and given me the strength to face the world each day, but you stood there beside me to face it with me. Lia, know that only you could have such a large and special place in my heart.

11 years ago I truly believe I was blessed by God and given an angel. Although you don't have wings, your heart has made mine better. I am a better person, and that I owe to you.

Smile to the future and know I love you from the bottom of my soul.

Bryan

CHAPTER 10

Out of Luck in America?

The health of the people is really the foundation upon which all their happiness and all their powers as a state depend.

—Benjamin Disraeli,
Earl of Beaconsfield (1804–1881)

Thankfully, throughout my ordeal, I did not have to worry about health insurance. My mom had worked in the health insurance business her entire career. She knew the ins and outs, forms and regulations, who to ask for what. In addition, Lia and I each had great health care coverage through our employers, and our insurance carrier covered Jeff's operation, too.

Many health insurance companies don't cover life-saving transplant operations involving a living donor unless the donor is a sibling. Lia and I were fortunate that our insurance did cover the majority of the total expenses. But it's not that way for everyone. My portion of the cost was a half a million dollars. If you don't have insurance or access to a lot of money, you're out of luck (at least, in America).

Once it's determined that a patient needs a transplant, most insurance companies have what they call "centers of excellence," which are medical centers or hospitals renowned for the type of transplant needed, where the insurance carrier prefers that the patient go for the operation. Fortunately for me, Tufts New England Medical Center was one such center of excellence in the transplant world. If it hadn't been, we would have had to pay outside of an insurance policy and would have had the burden of paying for additional expenses such as:

- **Travel and Lodging:** Lodging in Boston was very expensive. During our countless trips to and from the hospital, we didn't always want to make the more than two and a half hour drive home every night. Initially, one of Lia's friends who worked for Marriott Hotels gave us a few free stays and got us some "friends and family" rates. And then we discovered that a good portion of our lodging and travel had been covered in our policy all along.[35] That was another lesson learned the hard way: Ask every question imaginable about what your insurance policy does or does not cover, and read the fine print on your policy, no matter how fine the print is.

- **Lost Work Income:** When you're a patient in a hospital and can't work, you lose income. Many people in America aren't as fortunate as I was. Between my, Lia's and Jeff's employers, we were extremely lucky. Lia had started her new job in research at a pharmaceutical company just six months prior to my transplant and was able to take family leave.[36] Jeff was able to take short-term disability, receiving up to 75 percent of his pay for his lost work time.

- **Bankruptcy:** We had good insurance and we knew (and learned by experience) how to navigate the system. However, with the way the healthcare system is structured in the United States, it's not uncommon for people to have to literally file for bankruptcy, or sell or give up ownership of their home or property, just to receive the level of medical care and survive what major health catastrophes can inflict. Many people are forced to file for bankruptcy in order to qualify for government assistance in order to obtain necessary major medical care.

---

35. There was a $10,000 maximum, but you can spend that amount pretty quickly, on food, travel, gas and parking.
36. Which she and I both were allowed. The leave is unpaid (but at least you keep your job and your benefits).

Thank God for Lia's and my parents, our family, and supportive friends like Kelly McGuinness. Because of them, we didn't have to spend our way to destitution to save my life. We were the lucky ones, because if we didn't have all of that help and good insurance coverage, we would probably have lost our house, just so I could survive the crisis. But how does the average American put it all together when a loved one is in such dire need? What family has full insurance coverage, or an extra half a million dollars at their disposal these days? Many Americans are being swept under the rug—or worse—because they simply cannot afford health care insurance coverage.

Opportunities Reveal Character

When people show you who they are, believe them.

—Maya Angelou

I learned many lessons during my illness. One lesson was that I began to truly appreciate the importance of reaching out to people for help and encouragement. Fortunately for me, the vast majority of my relationships were positive and reinforced the good in people. I credit those relationships with carrying me through my weakest days.

However, while I witnessed the best of human nature during my time of greatest need, I also found myself confused and feeling let down by the worst of human nature. At the worst point during my battle against end-stage liver disease, just months before my transplant, I was abandoned by a lifelong friend. I was going to rely on him to handle some of my affairs, but he chose to walk away from me. It was a shock that I had to deal with this betrayal during the most vulnerable point in my life. Yet, as hurt as I was, I knew I had to consciously design a plan to handle relationships that take downturns at the worst possible times. It was an experience that reinforced my belief that my life depended on directing my focus, my thoughts and my time on people who genuinely cared about me. I knew I could not be consumed by this negative relationship situation, so I made a deliberate decision simply not to. There were times when I reluctantly had to give into being carried; but out of self-respect, I refused to allow people or situations to drag me down. It was crucial that my focus be on life, especially considering that mine was closer to ending than anyone knew.

This lesson was a great reminder of the need to protect one of our greatest assets: *positive thought*. While designing my "mindset plan," I decided that I had to let negative relationships go. It was a great moment of clarity for me. Mother Teresa once said, "Even God will not force us to do good. We must choose to do the good." I held no ill will, nor did I place blame on the person who let me down. I simply looked at it as a great lesson in life that forced me to develop a strategy that served me then, and will continue serving me into my future. I focused on the positive and on encouraging people in my life who wanted nothing more than to be a part of my fight to *win*. Everyone wants to be part of a winning team, but not everyone wants to be part of a team that might not win. I had to learn to build my team with people of great character, who knew there was a good chance I might not win this battle for my life. These were the type of people I surrounded myself with then and to this day. It wasn't about who I had known the longest; it was about who put their own objectives aside and stood up when others stepped away. These are the people who have my loyalty and respect.

To use the analogy of a boat whose ramp is beginning to lift, in life, there will be those people who run off the dock and leap onto the ramp without you if they think they might miss the boat. I have never been able to comprehend that way of thinking. The truth is, people who think that way have already missed the boat. Something that was instilled in me from a young age and was then reinforced in me once I joined the Marine Corps was to never leave someone behind. My "team," the people closest to me, who stuck by my side throughout my ordeal, innately understood this issue of loyalty without having to stop and consider it. It was just who they were.

The Ultimate Gift

Imagine the exponential "pay forward" effects on the world if more people would step up, put judgment and self interest aside, and choose to commit bold acts of unconditional giving. During my ordeal, my mother heard comments from some folks that, even after they died, they wouldn't allow their organs to be donated. One person even told her, "My husband won't let me donate my organs when I die." Why not? What is he going to use them for? We're not going to take our organs with us when we're gone. Why not save a life?

Most people don't give much thought to organ donations—until the issue of organ donation hits them personally. Until the need for a transplant strikes someone you know or love—a family member, a close friend, your next-door neighbor—we tend not to realize how urgent this issue is. Donating a liver is an exceptional act. You have a liver, you donate half, yours grows back in a few weeks, and you go on your merry way. Two people live.

I do understand that for a *living* donor, this is a highly personal issue. I would never try to convince somebody to donate this way, because if something happened to the donor, it would be tragic. Even if it turned out well, the donor would still have a scar forever. But having an advance directive[37] to be a donor in the event of sudden death is a different matter, because after you're gone . . . you're gone. Our organs are only taking us through this temporary journey of life. After that, we're either going to be cremated or buried. We're gone anyway, so why allow a perfectly good organ to rot when someone else's life might depend on it? Giving life while you're alive is the ultimate act of giving.

Without such an ultimate gift, I wouldn't be alive.

---

37. A medical advance directive can take the form of a donor card, a written statement by one's medical caregiver, or language in a will that in the event of death a person's organs are to be donated.

CHAPTER 11

What a Wonderful World

*It's good to be just plain happy; it's a little better to
know that you're happy; but to understand that you're
happy and to know why and how . . .
well, that is beyond happiness, that is bliss.*

—Henry Miller (1891–1980),
The Colossus of Maroussi

When I was diagnosed with a rare and deadly disease at the age of twenty-two, I felt as if my life's plans and desires were suddenly ripped out from under me. It turned out to be a long and difficult struggle, but I resolutely refused to let the disease get in my way or be a burden to others. Fortunately, I had an incredible amount of love and support from my family and friends; but it was only when I read what they had written in the Tufts New England Medical Center care pages during my time in the hospital, that I understood the strength and depth of my support system.

Looking back on it all, from when I was a perfectly healthy U.S. Marine, to the day that reality was shattered in an instant after being told I had only months to live, to where I have arrived now as I write these words, has been an absolute miracle. First, being directed to a particular specialist in Boston who knew how to keep me alive for eight years until I was given a liver. Then being dealt a devastating setback with the undiagnosed internal bleeding—which mysteriously stopped. Then having my original symptoms return—but by then, a radical new surgical procedure was available. It was an astounding journey. I had been forced to survive for so long—surviving the illness all the way until the transplant, surviving the transplant, surviving the first year after the transplant. Now I have gone from surviving to truly thriving in my life, to knowing that after I overcame all my setbacks, everything was okay and I could get on with my life.

A life I would not be living without the ultimate gift from Jeff Agli, whose liver I am proud to carry in me. Not without Lia, who stood by me year after year with steadfast love and encouragement.

Not without my parents, unwavering and relentless in giving me their all. Not without Kelly McGuinness, who cleared the decks and put walls of support and protection around me that enabled me to focus fully on the battle. It was their efforts and those of many other caring and supportive people who joined together to give me a second chance at the gift of life. These exceptional people made it possible for me to at last be able to really start my life.

I would also be forever indebted to Dr. Marshall Kaplan, the amazing doctor who had kept me alive against all odds for eight long years after I was supposed to have died; to Dr. Rohrer, who performed the transplant; to Dr. Freeman, who removed Jeff's liver and did my third surgery; and to Dr. Cooper, the surgeon who operated when I had the mysterious internal bleeding; and all of their support teams.

Now that it was all behind me and I had arrived at the beautiful light at the end of the long, dark tunnel, I sat down and wrote a very heartfelt letter . . .

> *To everyone,*
>
> *I would sign up for another eight years to get the same overwhelming feeling of love from all of you again. Thank you for your steadfast, endless support.*
>
> *And to Jeff: I recently got a card for someone that read, "You have faced an uphill battle and you are almost to the top. When this is over you will be on top and enjoy the remarkable vista." I can't think about you and keep my eyes dry. I can't thank you enough for your selfless act and only pray that I am worthy. I admire you and*

love you. I can't wait to share that vista with you. I'm not sure anyone ever asks to be a hero, but if anyone deserves that title it's you. I have always loved you for the person you are, the way that you take care of my sister and your two beautiful daughters. I have heard a lot of terms to describe you and I have used them myself, but those words truly cannot tell you the feeling I have for you for what you mean to me and for what you did for me. I don't remember what healthy is like or what a true good day felt like for many years . . . but thanks to you, I get to experience both of them again. I can only pray you feel the love I have for you and know how big of a place you have in my heart.

Thank you for my life.

Smile to the future and know I love you.

Love, Bryan.

* * *

Thanks to so many people, I am now "living large." In addition to being a loan officer at United Mortgage, I talk to groups and give motivational lectures on what my "death sentence" experience taught me about life, about the power of thought, about relationships.

I had not always been the outgoing, "public" person I am today. Before and during my ordeal, I was very private. For awhile after I was declared fit and healed, I remained a little self-protective and didn't want to give the power of thought over to

what I had battled against for so long. I didn't want to join myself
to anything that might bring back negative thoughts or memories. However, Jeff, Kristy and Lia soon started volunteering for
the Liver Foundation and various other fundraisers and walk-
a-thons. Yet, I held back. Then, gradually, it began to dawn on
me that it was the very power of thought that had protected me
and kept the steel in my resolve not to succumb to the terminal
illness in the first place . . . and that's when it struck me: I had a
lot to share! After all, I had won *life*.

To the shock and surprise of my family and friends, I began
to open up. I started going out and telling people all about my
eight-year battle. Something was sparking me to use my story
to motivate people, to make them feel better, to give them hope.
I began to go on the liver walks, to volunteer, and to speak before
groups. It was an extreme metamorphosis for me to go from being
contained and private to being open, outgoing and expressive with
strangers. And I loved it. The caterpillar was out of the cocoon. I
didn't want attention on myself, I just wanted people to know that,
like the Chris Isaac song says, "everything's going to be alright."

What had prompted me to change was a special gift that Lia
and I had received . . .

The Gift

Around the time Lia and I were told that we may never have children of our own, she was already pregnant with our baby. We
named her "Lily J.," who is now a beautiful three year old little
splash of life, with the budding beauty of her mother and the
determined drive of her father. She is a blessing, a sparkle, the
sweetest, most loving, outgoing little girl on Earth. My eyes fill

with tears, knowing she would not be here without Jeff's gift and without my decision to stay positive and to win my life.

There are dads who don't do much with their children. But being a father after what I experienced gave me the realization that *time is fleeting*. Each minute that passes by is a minute gone forever. It can't be undone, it can't be re-lived. It's over. I take time with Lily. When she was young, I changed her diapers. I played with her. I make dinner for her and Lia every night (Lia gets home from work later than I do). Lily was well worth every minute of the eight years of pain and suffering I endured. And the "J" in her name? It stands for "Jeff"—a selfless hero the likes of which this world rarely gets the privilege of being blessed with.

My mother always said, "Nothing is guaranteed in life." I have learned well that those words are true. Nobody has ever proven that I won't get PSC again. That thought alone will make a man slow down and enjoy his family, his friends, his life, to smell the roses, to love unconditionally, to pour himself into the lives of others. It's also not known if PSC is genetic. But I do know this: I have Lily's blood type and she is welcome to my liver any time if she ever needs it. That, I guarantee.

So, the next time somebody tells you, *You can't, You won't, You don't, You shouldn't, You'll never*, tell them this: "Bryan and Lia Donahue's little girl is named Lily. They weren't supposed to be able to have her. In fact, Bryan was supposed to be dead years ago."

What else can I say? I married the girl of my dreams. My daughter is more than I could have ever asked for. I am alive and well.

Poet and author Linda Ellis wrote a book titled *The Dash*, in which she succinctly described the path of life. The beginning and ending verses tell it all: "I read of a man who stood to speak at

155

the funeral of a friend. He referred to the dates on her tombstone from the beginning—to the end. . . . So when your eulogy is being read, with your life's actions to rehash, would you be proud of the things they say . . . about how you spent your dash?"[38]

Today, I am somewhere in the middle of my dash. And it is a dream come true.

Hopefully, I will not be writing any more letters like the ones my illness prompted me to have to write. But there is one letter I will always cherish. I often read it in the late hours when I want to be reminded of what life is really all about. The letter was written many years ago, before I was diagnosed with PSC, before precious little Lily J. Donahue was born, way back in college, when I was a single man, in search of my princess . . .

To Bryan,

When I looked at you I wondered
I tingled inside
You made me feel wanted and happy
You were my escape
As I grew to know you
Our feelings were kept hidden
I denied what I felt
Yet I knew something was there
We both kept everything inside
Yet we had so much to say
As time goes on I grow more comfortable
And you make me feel this way
You teach me things and open my eyes
You make me feel safe and secure

---

38. Linda Ellis, *The Dash: Making a Difference with Your Life* (Simple Truths, 2006), p.38.

I laugh like I never laughed before
You're like the sun chasing all the rain away
I think about you, I want to talk to you
I hear your voice and I want to be with you
I see you and I want to hug you, kiss you, and wrap my
*   arms around you*
I dream about you when I sleep and I long to wake up in
*   your arms*
Words cannot express
the feelings that I hold for you
As I remember all of our memories together
And as I think ahead to our future
my body grows weak
as a rush of love flows through my veins
The cloud of love that surrounds you
as you stand by my side
makes me want to never let you go
In the friendship that we share
and as our love continues to grow
Always know that you are my best friend
*And that I will **always** love you.*

. . . Lia

EPILOGUE:
Life Lessons Learned

America loves a winner . . . . Americans play to win.

—General George S. Patton, Jr.[39]

Through my ordeal, the lessons I learned and the wisdom I gained in less than the space of a decade were about as much as I would have thought I'd learn in a lifetime. One of the biggest things I learned was the power of family. The support of my family was immeasurable. We circled the wagons, we worked through it, we never gave up. Everybody drew together, kept all negative out, kept naysayers away, and were there for each other. Together, we won.

After he retired from the U.S. Postal Service in 2009,[40] three years after my transplant, my father, upon reflecting on his life,

---

39.   Giving his troops a final pep-talk prior to the invasion of Normandy; Enniskillen Manor Grounds, England, May 17, 1944.

40.   For many years, my father had been on the road constantly, traveling all over the nation. The job was wearing him out. In 2009, he retired from the postal service. In a career that had spanned nearly four decades, he'd worked his way up the ranks from clerk, letter carrier and maintenance mechanic, all the way to the position he was retiring from, the top man in charge as the Northeast Area Security Coordinator (which encompassed the New England states and New York, to the Canadian border). By then, he had complete access to all post office buildings and vehicles. In fact, just prior to the tragic events of 9/11, he was part of a team that conducted a security assessment of all postal police operations throughout the country for the Postal Inspection Service in Washington D.C.

said, "I've got a great wife. All of my kids are educated. They've all got great spouses. They all own their own houses. They all have great kids. I'm retired. I have six granddaughters and can walk to any of their houses and see them any day. I have the best wife a man could ever dream of. . . . I am the luckiest person I know."

I respectfully disagree that it was luck. It was actually my dad's character—something in him as a man and as a father—and a decision he made early on to break the chain of his upbringing and be a better dad to his children than his dad had been. My father made wise choices, worked hard, and was shown good examples. For instance, as a young Marine after he returned from Vietnam, he learned through a foundation of examples set for him through the family of his young wife, my mother. Every Sunday, he would go to her house and join her family for their weekly dinner, where he would observe how respectfully her father treated everyone, how people honored him, and how his wife (my grandmother) helped create a joyful, solid and caring family atmosphere.

No, it was no accident how I turned out; my father and mother had everything to do with it. There was something in them—spine, love, honor and grace—that helped create and build who I am, and who I'm still growing into every day.

And so, just as that young Marine left the horrors of Vietnam and built a new life, I too left the horrors of PSC and got busy building my new life. In the process, as I reflected on life's lessons learned, I began to see people from a new vantage point.

A Different Perspective

One thing I became painfully aware of during my time of learning was that I had to admit that too often I was no saint. Part of my

160

desire to grow was the courage to be able to take a hard look at myself, honestly identify areas in me that needed improvement, and then work on them. The revelations were astounding. If you've ever had to be around someone you don't get along with, then you know what I mean. But I began to realize that more often than not in situations like those, it was usually based on an unexamined misperception, and that each person was at least half of the problem.

So I came up with a way to deal with those types of situations from an entirely new perspective. When meeting someone for the first time, it's human nature to form an initial impression of them. So the next time I met someone new, I tried a little exercise. I chose someone in my life who made me smile, who made me feel like the most important person in the world: my little daughter Lily. To prevent myself from instilling in my mind the wrong impression of someone before I got to know them, I would imagine Lily's head on their body. Sounds funny—I know. But this way, with the person I was just meeting, our relationship would get off to a great start. This little trick pulled down my walls and allowed me to get to know the person before I decided if I wanted them in my life. It also worked with people I already knew. I found that I began to treat them better—and they noticed it!

I tried this with a coworker in my office whom I had known for years. There were many times when she just drove me nuts. I was stressed out about our lack of relationship. We communicated differently. We handled things differently. We looked at things differently. (Yet, regardless of how our conversations went, or how stressful I felt that the tension had been between us on any given day, the very next day she acted as if it had never happened; and she never held it against me.) I did everything I could to find a logical solution to the impasse. It never came, because I had been looking for an answer to magically appear that was not there—and would never be there *unless I changed **my** perspective*. So I began to speculate. *What if I'm the one with the sour attitude and she's just being super nice and keeping her mouth shut about me?* Was I the one who was actually causing the stress and strain in our relationship? It was when I pictured Lily's face on her and focused on the spirit of everything this woman did, that something in me began to lift. I started to realize that I could have been more patient, more understanding, more caring toward her. I looked at the "heart" of everything she did, who she was, where she was coming from . . . and it dawned on me that all along, at the core of all she did was her desire to protect and serve us.

The reality was that she had a great attitude. I just didn't see it, because my expectations of her blocked my perception of the *intentions of her heart*. I was missing this before because I was focused on the things that annoyed me (and judging *her* for them all!). I was embarrassed that I had been so dismissive to this kind lady who only had my best interests at heart all along. And even though she perceived me as a crab, she always smiled and put up with me!

She had no idea that I had been testing my theory on her by imagining Lily's head on her shoulders. Within a few days of my putting the idea into practice with her, she went to our boss Kelly and said, "Bryan seems to be much happier lately." She was right! Because I had changed my attitude and began to see her as she actually was. Now I walk out of the elevator at the office with a smile and I know there will be an equally big one waiting for me. The best part is that she doesn't hold my previous crabbiness against me.

None of this had been obvious to me until I changed my perspective and looked at her from a nonjudgmental point of view. I learned to focus on people's positive attributes and let the negatives go. This lesson taught me that if I'm experiencing a problem with another person, I never judge until I look at myself first, to see if I might be part of the problem. And if I am the problem, then I *change*.

Rolling with the Tough Times

If your ship doesn't come in, swim out to meet it!

—Jonathan Winters

As 2008 descended on America, with the collapse in the housing market and real estate mortgage business, I decided to seek greener pastures because I was beginning to feel inadequate to deal with the flood of changes that were happening in my industry. I had come into the business during the boom years, when lending was footloose and fancy-free. People like Kelly had experience lending under the stricter guidelines of years earlier, so she was accustomed to the changes. But by 2009, the "return to reason" that began to come over the home loan industry was difficult for me to deal with, because I'd never loaned that way before, with such rigid structure and endless guidelines. I had come in before the financial collapse, when things were easy, when standards for mortgage approvals weren't as tough as in previous decades. During this new, post-collapse period, however, the guidelines were tightening up and changing literally every day—which meant that I was constantly changing what I was telling customers.

That was tough for me as a man of principle, a man of his word. It was important to me, as a person who took my profession seriously, that if I had told somebody their loan was okay, then I wanted to be able to mean exactly that. It was a big adjustment for me to have to pull back on my word, even if it was solely due to the changing nature of the business in those heady years of 2008 through 2010, when things were all over the map with the economy and the real estate business. For me to tell a customer they were all set and everything looked good with their loan, and then within weeks or days (because lending guidelines were changing so rapidly) to have to tell them things had changed was huge, because I had given my word.

I would go to bed at night stressed out about a deal and it would eat away at me. And then I woke up in the middle of the night one night during a particular loan situation that was getting away from me and I remembered my own credo: "When I let the problem become bigger than me, I lose." That was exactly what I was doing—losing all these battles because I had allowed the problem to balloon out of control until it was controlling me. Even though Kelly McGuinness patiently explained to me from her experience how the industry goes through periods of ebb and flow, it took awhile for me to get comfortable with the fact that the whole business was changing right beneath me. Once I finally began to realize that it was industry-wide, that it was just the evolution of the business, I was able to adjust my expectations and get back in control of my career and better manage my customers' expectations.

Even during the tough times, it is important to remember that we are in charge of our thought processes, our mental attitudes, our challenges in life. I stretched my comfort zone and made a mental shift, based on the idea that I was the only one to blame for my success or failure; and if I could control whether I succeeded or failed, then I had control over my entire life. Having people like Kelly around me made all the difference in keeping my mental compass on target.

We all experience setbacks in life. How our setbacks turn out depends entirely on how we deal with them. My setback drove home how precious life was. I was literally on my death bed two times in two months. You can't get set back much farther than that. So I had to dig deeper and keep in mind that I would get beyond my challenges if I stayed positive and had an optimistic plan to focus on. Now, I no longer stress about the past; instead, I use the past to look at myself, to see where I could have done better and where and how I can improve.

It's All in Our Choices

Life is a series of little choices that can wind up putting us on a great path or a less than great path—which is why we need to learn to make choices that set us up to win. Life can be a "crap shoot," but we can increase our odds of success and minimize our risk of failure. There have been several simple choices I've made in life that, had I *not* made them, could have had a major impact on my life. For example, not marrying Lia. Or deciding not to go to work at United Mortgage. Or deciding not to travel to Boston to see the medical specialists. Each of those choices I made was deliberate, and each of them was a brick in the road that led to saving my life—and then making it richer, more productive, and more amazing.

The biggest thing that helped me with every decision I made was that I made these decisions after looking into all of my options. For example, with Lia, I dated her, got to know her, met her family, grew to love her, and knew that she loved me. There was never a doubt in my mind. Asking her to marry me was an obvious decision for me to make (and probably one of the best decisions I'll ever make). Or my decision to work at United Mortgage. Before accepting their offer, I looked at the company as a whole, I looked at the people who were running it, and even asked to speak to some employees after my last interview before they offered me the job so I could hear from them what they thought—and I heard a lot of the same: "Great company." "Won't find better people." That made it an easy decision for me.

A life is built on choices. I am writing these words today only because I chose in 1998 to focus on winning my days and staying positive. Whether I admitted it back then or not, I was held back with my liver problem. At times, it seemed easier to give in. But I realized that if I didn't focus on the positive, then the negative would swoop in and fill that void. Once I got into a daily rhythm of choosing to be positive, it was much easier to keep the negative at bay. Now, I refuse to even think things like, *What if the PSC disease returns?* It's true; there is a statistical chance that it could return at the ten-year post-operation point. So what? I could die from any number of other things before that. I learned not to cower under the "what ifs," but to focus on the things that *create a great* life. That mindset is a choice.

I learned to deliberately appreciate life, to stop and smell the roses. To always be aware that we get only one chance at life.

A Positive Mindset

Here are three homework exercises that I recommend you try, to improve your outlook on life:

1. THE RULE OF REALISTIC GOALS: Your future success is limited only by your expectations and desires. Don't be held back by a preconceived thought that you "couldn't" or "shouldn't." You will not achieve fulfillment if you set low expectations. Live your dream, go BIG, aim high. When you set your goals too low and achieve them, then you actually fail. Don't set realistic goals; set goals that you would only dream about. That way, even if you don't hit your highest goals, you'll still be successful.

   Your assignment: Re-evaluate your professional and personal goals. Be honest with yourself. If your goals are realistic, throw them out! Set goals that you would dream about. Grade yourself on the shift you make mentally and how that makes you feel, based on your happiness and sense of achievement.

2. THE RULE OF REGRET: If you feel you might soon regret something you could have done one day but didn't, then do it right then and there. Decide that you will never again experience a time when you are on the fence about something you wanted to do but weren't sure if you should or could do it—only to realize that when you decided not to do it, you regretted it. Live in the NOW as often as realistically possible (given your circumstances). Choose to immerse yourself in those "once-in-a-lifetime" experiences as they present themselves—even if it's just the little everyday things that people tend to take for granted, such as spending a few extra minutes with loved ones instead of extra time at work.

   Your assignment: Think back over the last year about something you wanted to do but never did it. Force yourself to make it happen *this weekend*. If you are fortunate enough that you do not have any regrets over the last year, then do something you have never done before.

3. THE RULE OF TOP 3: I once heard Kelly say, "On my speed dial of people, Bryan is in the top three. If the chips are down, he's the guy I'm calling." We should all have a Top 3 List, people we can call on 24/7/365 who won't ask questions; they'll just hit the road for us. These are the people you would want in your corner when things go bad.

   Your assignment: If you don't have people like Kelly McGuinness in your life, find them. Have a discussion with someone you trust about them being there to support you if you need them in the tough times. Surround yourself with these positive people. If you ask with your heart in the right place, they'll see it. You'll be giving them a gift, too: your unhesitating trust and loyalty in return.

My illness helped me to build character and to appreciate life. It made me realize that when I was sick and fighting to live, the results were contingent on my showing up for the battle with a determined attitude. It's the same for each of us: If you choose to succeed, *only **you** can stop you.*

We all have bad days. We simply need to choose to deal with them and control them. The best part about a bad day is that *we actually **can** change it*. You **can** flip the switch and win. If you are having a bad day, then find like-minded, positive people who will snap you out of it and help you re-center yourself so you can focus on the positive. The minute you wake up each morning, deliberately decide that you are going to **win that day.** Remember, when you are bigger than your problem, you control it. It is when you let that problem become bigger than you, that you will lose.

The power of thought is only limited to what you can imagine. In fact, we become what we think most often about ourselves, because *thought creates*. That's why it's crucial that we take responsibility for our thoughts and actions. Failure is temporary—but quitting makes it permanent. Winning starts in the mind. Sound simplistic? It is. It's called *will power*—the will of the mind. It's a *mindset* of choice and determination. I know, because I did it every day for eight years. And I still do it today. After I had finally gotten back to work, my first month became my most productive month ever. Because from the minute I woke up each day, I chose to make that day a good day. After all, I was alive! I had cheated death. And you can't get much closer to death than I had been.

In his book, *The Magic of Thinking Big*, author David J. Schwartz, wrote, "The size of your success is determined by the size of your belief. Think little goals and expect little achievements. Think big goals and win big success. Big ideas and big plans are often easier—certainly no more difficult—than small ideas and small plans."

My hope is that my story has been an inspirational one that will help, inspire and encourage you—regardless of your current situation, or how your future might look to you right now. Your future can be as great as you allow it to be. You *can* change your negative circumstances—and that change can alter your entire life.

If you are reading these words, then at least you are breathing. But are you really *living*? It's up to you to get out there and *choose to live*. It starts in your mind: It's the power of thought.

About the Authors

Bryan Donahue lives in North Haven, Connecticut, with his wife Lia; daughter, Lily and dog, Lucy. He is a loan officer at United Mortgage, in North Haven, and he gives motivational lectures about the power of thought in creating a productive, fulfilling and successful life.

His website can be seen at: www.Brdonahue.com

Bryan may be contacted at: Bryan@Brdonahue.com

Author M. Rutledge McCall lives in southern California and has ghostwritten, and or edited, scores of books for dozens of published authors worldwide. His nonfiction book, *Slipping Into Darkness: A True Story From the American Ghetto*, was published to international acclaim, and is currently being developed as a motion picture.

His credentials may be viewed at: www.Linkedin.com/in/MRutledgeMcCall

McCall may be contacted at: McCall@MRutledgeMcCall.com